THE ART OF COURAGEOUS LIVING

JOHN A. O'BRIEN

New York

McMULLEN BOOKS, INC.

1950

I

Contents

Page

How to Read This Book Most Profitably

To get the most help *from this book, read but one chapter a day. Each chapter presents an important principle for the conquest of needless fear and anxiety, and illustrates it with a number of incidents.*

Reflect upon the principle for five minutes. Use it in confronting and analyzing any fear or anxiety disturbing you.

Write out your thoughts and feelings concerning the disturbing situation. Then review your notes. You will thus be enabled to locate the source of anxiety. Deal with it calmly, intelligently, and effectively.

Remember that anxiety merely disturbs and weakens you. Instead of helping you to solve a problem, it hinders you. This is true of all emotions. Problems can be solved only by thinking. The calmer you are, the clearer and more effective is your thinking. The most rewarding of all activity is calm, clear thinking.

Reflect upon the incidents illustrating the principle developed in each chapter. See if you can't capture the spirit behind each deed of courage and apply it to your daily tasks.

Since books were first written and lectures were first delivered, every reader and listener will testify that the concrete incident, the story, lingers in the mind long after the abstract theory or principle has faded. Because each chapter is replete with stories which inspire courage and remain vividly in the mind, the reader will derive the greatest help and inspiration and secure the maximum of assimilation of both thought and spirit if he contents himself with the perusal of but one chapter a day till the book is finished.

Then read the volume in this way once a month for the first year and quarterly thereafter. Since fears and anxieties, like hardy perennials, arise to disturb one's serenity as long as life lasts, there will always remain the need of reading a book showing how to deal with fear and to develop courage.

John A. O'Brien

THE ART OF COURAGEOUS LIVING

"Courage conquers all things" — Ovid

CHAPTER ONE

THE NATURE OF COURAGE

Gloucester, 'tis true that we are in great danger,
The greater therefore should our courage be.
—Shakespeare, *Henry V*

THE NEED OF THE WORLD *today is courage. The worry and fear caused by a world war and the uncertainty as to what is in store for us in the postwar world have eaten like acids into the marrow of mankind. No individual has escaped the tidal wave of concern, fear and anxiety which has swept the face of the earth. Wistfully, millions are saying: "IF I had courage!"—only to bemoan their lack of it. Neurasthenia is the distemper of the day.*

Worry is debilitating. Fear paralyzes the springs of action. The need for a remedy that will release soul and body from the grip of these twin evils is the paramount need of our day. That remedy is the iron virtue of courage. It is the magic alchemist which transforms a person, trembling and scared half to death, into a valiant hero. It enables a person to surmount difficulties, to rise upon the ladder of handicaps, and to turn obstacles into stepping stones.

Without courage, no equipment will prevail. With courage, the thinnest armor takes on double thickness and strength. "What a new face," observes Emerson, "courage puts on everything!" Suddenly, the worst turns to the best for the brave.

This work is designed to show how fear may be overcome and courage may be developed. It does this in two ways. First, it shows the conditions which breed fear and the attitudes which beget courage. It avails itself of the latest findings of modern science. Second, it presents abundant examples of bravery from all walks in life. These instances, vivid and graphic, engender an atmosphere of stout-heartedness which is bound to infect the reader. We believe that no person can read this book without rising up from his chair with the determination to face life and all its difficulties with the courage to win through to victory.

Universally Admired

Of all the qualities of character which provoke the admiration of men, there are few which do so with such spontaneity and universality as that of courage. It makes an appeal to something deep in human nature which neither friend nor foe can resist. Regardless of the changes of fashion in human conduct, courage is never outmoded. Its appeal is time-less, changeless, and universal. If moderation may be said to be the silken thread running through all the virtues, courage may be said to be the foundation of all. For, as Sir James M. Barrie has observed, "All goes, if courage goes." Similar is the conviction of Doctor Johnson: "Unless a man has that virtue, he has no security for preserving any other."

Like the hardy perennial that shoots forth its blossoms not only amidst the soft zephyrs of May but also amidst the blustery winds of December, courage has blossomed in every season of the race's history and knows no limitations of border or race. It is the monopoly of no race, the heritage of no tribe. Its fatherland is the earth and all men are its potential heirs.

In the mythology of every race there is a Hector, a Hercules, an Achilles, a Beowulf, an Arthur, a Lancelot, a Cid. In the authentic history of every people there is an Alexander, an Horatio, a Leonidas, a Caesar, a Richard the Lion-Hearted, a Napoleon, a Foch, a Robert Emmett, a Stonewall Jackson, a Rickenbacker, a MacArthur, a Colin Kelly. Their likenesses are perpetuated in statues and paintings; their names are enshrined in song and story; their memories live in the heart-throbs of the race. In the melodies that lilt the story of their fame, the recurring overtone is that of courage under fire, of gallantry in the face of impending doom. It is that quality which makes the heart beat faster, provokes its meed of admiration from friend and foe, and anchors its possessors securely on the pedestals carved for the heroes of the race.

Although it is so highly prized in every land, courage is not a common virtue. The feet of most men are weighted with the lead of fear. "Mankind," observes Benjamin Franklin, "are dastardly when they meet with opposition." It was none other than a general, Lord Wellington, who declared: "Uniforms were often masks." Most men shy away from danger as instinctively as a horse shies away from an unfamiliar object in the road. The generality of mankind is quite content to plod safely along the middle of the road, leaving the edges of the gulleys and the brinks of the precipices to more venturesome and fearless spirits.

Need of our Day

The dominant need of our day is courage. Courage for the fields of endeavor which encircle the globe, embrace the waters of the deep, and reach into the skies of all the world. Courage for the herculean task of building a new and better world out of the ruins of the old. Courage for the task of preserving our clearness of vision, our capacity for calm thinking, and the control of our emotions, instead of yielding to hysteria and frenzy. The building of a world organization that will relegate war to the limbo of outmoded institutions demands that we "screw our courage to the sticking place."

It will be worth while, therefore, to look deeply into the nature of this crucial and all-important virtue of courage, to examine its various kinds and to discover how it may be developed in greater measure by all of us. A calm and reasoned probing of the factors conditioning its emergence and sustaining its vitality and vigor, and the means of anchoring it in our souls until the journey's end, would seem to be one of the necessary antecedents for successful living today.

Far from stripping this heroic virtue of its glamor and unique appeal, this peering into its face will, we think, increase our admiration and deepen our determination to develop it in our own souls. Even though we walk not on the mountain peaks but in the valleys, we can still be heroes, worthy of the highest acclaim. Indeed, it is to the perfection of heroes and saints that even the humblest of us are called. Addressed to every human being are the words of the Master: "Be you therefore perfect, as also your heavenly Father is perfect." Central in the composite of qualities constituting perfection is courage.

Courage is a quality of the mind which enables one to meet danger and difficulties with firmness and valor. It implies a subordination of fear or pain to a fixed purpose or a steadfast resolution. Bravery is daring, often defiant, courage. Boldness is the antithesis of timidity. Dauntlessness connotes courage of a lofty and unintimidated character. Gallantry implies a dashing and adventurous courage. Fortitude is passive courage, especially in the endurance of pain or adversity. Heroism is a contempt of danger from a noble and self-forgetful devotion. At the opposite pole from courage is cowardice.

Courage Has Eyes

Courage is never to be confused with recklessness, which is lacking in prudent caution. Courage must have eyes as well as hands and feet. That is a high type of courage which first measures the formidableness of the danger and then takes effective means to cope with it. Not without purpose has the sense of fear been rooted in the race; prudent fear is the beginning of wisdom as it is of courage. Not long would we live if the inhibitions of prudent fear were removed from us. "Courage," points out Fenelon, "is a virtue only as far as it is directed by prudence." Joanna Baillie states the case well:

The brave man is not he who feels no fear,
For that were stupid and irrational;

But he, whose noble soul its fear subdues,
And bravely dares the danger nature shrinks from.

The results of a scientific investigation of fear, conducted under the direction of the National Research Council, were published in the authoritative *Infantry Journal.** The study shows that fear is nature's method of mobilizing in an all-out way for an all-out emergency: it pulls all the body's resources into a state of preparedness for an ordeal. Fear in the form of prudent concern increases strength and endurance.

There are a few men in every army, the study discloses, who know no fear. Fortunately, just a few. For such individuals are not normal. They would be readily recognized by a psychiatrist as mentally deficient. Their callousness of mind makes them incapable of emotion, and hence incapable of fear; their lack of wholesome inhibitions of prudent fear makes them tend toward mere recklessness. Great accomplishments, calling for sustained courage and intelligence, are achieved by normal men who have learned to subjugate their fear for causes worthwhile.

"They say it takes a guy too dumb to be scared," replied Capt. Joseph J. Foss, when asked what it felt like thousands of feet high in a plane with enemy bullets whizzing around him. He had just shot down his twenty-sixth enemy plane over Guadalcanal, equalling Rickenbacker's record in World War I. "But any guy," continued Joe, "that says he isn't scared when bullets start coming through his plane is a darn liar."

Courage and fear are not opposites. Courage does not

---

* January, 1943.

mean the absence of fear, but its subordination to a steadfast resolution. Marshal Ney offers a good illustration of this. His courage was a byword among his soldiers; his conduct during the retreat from Moscow was a magnificent demonstration of the driving power of an indomitable will rising above all hardships. Napoleon called him the bravest of the brave.

Was Ney without fear? Far from it. On the morning at Waterloo, his knees trembled so much that he had difficulty in climbing into his saddle. Looking down contemptuously at those shaking knees, Ney shouted: "Shake away, knees! You would shake worse than that if you knew where I was going to take you!"

That day, five horses were shot under him. Here was the resolute direction of the body and its members, whether docile or unruly, whether inclined or disinclined, from the conning tower of the mind. Certain tremors and sensations of the body arise involuntarily, but the courageous man will not be dictated to by them: He will dictate to them, and bring them under subjection. That is all that can be asked of any man. The coward is one who has never learned to master his fears, but who allows them habitually to run away with him.

Courage Lighted by Reason

Too much stress cannot be placed upon the fact that prudence and courage walk hand in hand, and are never to be viewed as pulling in opposite directions. The man who takes risks needlessly and without due preparation is not courageous, but rash. Far, then, from acting without the guidance of reason, courage utilizes all the light to chart its way and then plunges resolutely onward. "Be sure you are right," cautioned Lincoln, "*then* go ahead." His appeal was for courage lighted by reason—the most commendable and fruitful kind of courage.

If the weighing of the *pros* and *cons* be carried on too lengthily, the capacity of decision becomes sicklied o'er with the pale cast of thought. Caution degenerates into overcautiousness; timidity paralyzes the springs of action; the will is hamstrung into a state of chronic indecision which psychologists call abulia. Who has not known a pathetic individual who is forever unable to make up his mind, who is perpetually answering "yes" and "no" and meaning neither?

The fact of the matter is that, after all the consequences are carefully weighed, vacillation should yield to decision and action. Courage is required in every decision: nothing ventured nothing gained. There is no crown without its cross; there is no prize without a struggle; no victory without a contest.

> *And he is dead who will not fight*
> *And who dies fighting has increase.*

"The greatest glory that has ever come to me," observed Sir James M. Barrie when he was an old man, "was to be swallowed up in London, not knowing a soul, with no means of subsistence, and the fun of working till the stars went out."

When Francisco Pizzaro was about to undertake his epochal march down the west coast of South America to carve out of the uncharted wilderness a New Spain, he heard that some of his followers were murmuring at the prospect of the dangers before them. Taking his sword, Pizzaro drew a line on the sand from east to west. Then turning toward the south, he said: "Friends and comrades! On that side are toil, hunger, nakedness, the drenching storm, desertion, and death. On this side, ease and pleasure. There lies Peru with its riches; here, Panama and its poverty. Choose, each man, what best becomes a brave Castilian. For my part I go to the south!"

So saying, he stepped across the line. Thirteen others followed his example, thus showing their willingness to abide the fortunes of their leader, come what may. "Fame," to quote the words of an ancient chronicler, "has commemorated the name of the little band, who thus, in the face of difficulties unexampled in history, with death rather than riches for their reward, preferred all to abandoning their honor, and stood firm by their leader as an example of loyalty to future ages."

Courage was in the blood of those hardy adventurers and they needed but the challenge to have it come to the surface. Daring explorers, they blazed a path through the wilderness that mankind has been following ever since. New continents are not discovered by timid souls. Men leave the comforts of home to explore the Antarctic. Like Shakespeare's soldier, they still seek

. . . . the bubble reputation
Even in the cannon's mouth.

Provoke Admiration from Foe

It is interesting to note that exhibitions of courage and daring provoke admiration even from the enemy. While I was at Oxford, the news came that a German U-boat captain had maneuvered his craft through all the network of chains and mines into the mouth of the harbor Scapa Flow and sunk the aircraft carrier, *Ark Royal,* while it was resting at anchor. It was sad news to the British people, but it was an amazing feat for the U-boat. In announcing the loss, Churchill, then Chief Lord of the Admiralty, paid tribute to the courage and skill of that captain. Courage of friend or foe seems to strike a spot in the human heart which renders it impossible for one to withhold his admiration: respect for courage outstrips nationality and self-interest and is coextensive with human kind.

Why does courage provoke its meed of admiration even from the adversary who succumbs before it? Deploring his own defeat, he yet finds himself *compelled* to admire the courage and daring which enables his opponent to mount the shining peak of victory. Is it not because deep down in the hidden depths of the human soul there is the universal conviction that there are values which far transcend one's own self-interest, and which are worth risking one's own personal welfare and life to achieve?

Lt. John James Powers, but a few months out of the choir of his parish church in Brooklyn, gave striking illustration of this truth in his fighting in the Coral Sea. During the first two days, Lieutenant Powers, piloting a dive-bomber in the face of blasting enemy fire, destroyed one large enemy gunboat, put a second out of commission, severely damaged an aircraft tender and a 20,000-ton transport, and scored a direct hit on an aircraft carrier which burst into flames and sank shortly after.

On the morning of the third day, Lieutenant Powers remarked to the pilots of his squadron as they were about to climb into their planes: "Remember, the folks back home are counting on us. I am going to get a hit if I have to lay it on their flight deck."

Leading his section down to the target from an altitude of 18,000 feet, he dove through a screen of bursting anti-aircraft shells and enemy planes until he almost touched the deck. Not till then did he release his bomb. So sure did he want to be of a direct hit.

He was last seen, reported President Roosevelt (in posthumously awarding him the Medal of Honor), attempting recovery from his dive at the extremely low altitude of 200 feet, amid a terrific barrage of shell and bomb fragments, smoke, flame, and debris from the stricken vessel. His plane was shattered by the explosion of his own bomb; but he had made good his promise to "lay it on the flight deck." Through death's open door he plunged into a glory that knows no death. To this slender young choir boy we may apply the words of Shakespeare: "He hath borne himself beyond the promise of his age, doing in the figure of a lamb, the feats of a lion."

Diving into almost certain death, Lt. John James Powers gave dramatic expression to the belief that there are causes which far transcend one's comfort and safety. A noble cause towers above the self-interest of the individual as the snow-capped Jungfrau towers above the lowly foot-hills. This is the truth which the Master proclaimed when He said: "For he that will save his life, shall lose it: and he that shall lose his life for my sake, shall find it." In that paradox is expressed the central truth of the Christian gospel and the key to the understanding of all the heroic sacrifices for truth, justice, and righteousness since the world began.

It was of this truth which the great poet, A. E. Housman, in a lecture at Cambridge in 1933 declared: "That is the most important truth which has ever been uttered, and the greatest discovery ever made in the moral world." In the cheerful willingness to face danger, hardship, suffering, death itself for a cause which transcends one's own self-interest, is found the hidden core of that inner compulsion forcing all men to pay tribute to the courage and daring of friend and foe.

The Sense of Self-Preservation

That is doubtless why we find ourselves withholding admiration and looking somewhat scornfully upon the person who sets too high a premium upon his own self-interest when compared with the public weal. As with a sixth sense we discern a certain pusillanimity in the exaggerated sense of self-importance in the individual who is in the chronic attitude of thinking of himself and of his own petty interests first, and only secondly, if at all, of the welfare of society. The sense of self-preservation can be developed to the extent that the universe is regarded as existing for the one solitary purpose of providing for the ease, security, and comfort of oneself, while the feeling for others becomes blurred and vestigial. Such an attitude, even when dimly felt, never fails to provoke an unfavorable reaction.

The Irish poet, Padraic Colum, quotes an illuminating observation of Yeats on this point. "Once," relates Colum, "when I was walking down a street in Dublin, John Butler Yeats said to me, 'Our liking for people is in inverse ratio to their sense of self-preservation,' and this saying explained to me why certain very admirable people are often not warmly liked by us—their sense of self-preservation obscurely realized by us diminishes the liking we might expect to have for them. And then I thought that it needs a dramatic confrontation to show us that no matter how admirable certain people of importance may be, they have not a character that we can truly venerate and love, since they lack the quality which over-balances their sense of self-preservation."

We find it necessary, however, to qualify the above generalization. We do not find anything objectionable in a strong sense of self-preservation in contending with the daily vicissitudes of modern life; we find it rational and wholly admirable. It is the goal of the innumerable campaigns which railroads, factories, automobile associations, insurance companies and public welfare agencies find necessary to institute to cut down the enormous toll of accidents, now killing or maiming a person every few seconds of the day and night.

It is only when the individual is unwilling to subordinate that sense of self-preservation for a risk to be undertaken in the public welfare that objection can be reasonably lodged. Performers who scale the front of public buildings, or who dance or turn somersaults upon the narrow peaks of such edifices, can usually attract a crowd of curious gapers; but we find little or nothing to admire in such exhibitions. In fact, we usually find ourselves turning away from them with something like resentment for the foolish risking of life and limb; it strikes us as irrational, stupid, and immoral. They leave with us the impression of show-offs—vulgar exhibitionists pandering to a morbid public.

Daredeviltry or Courage

True courage, therefore, is anchored in reason; it is educated fear; it assumes risks only for causes worth while. It demands a *quid pro quo*—a justification and a compensation for a risk. It leaves to the so-called dare-devil the reckless assumption of risks of life and limb for vainglorious exhibitionism. Because they are fundamentally stupid and irrational, mere recklessness and daredeviltry are unworthy of the respect and admiration so universally accorded to true courage. This fact is recognized in the laws which exist in most communities forbidding reckless risks, which are veerings to suicide and not infrequently reach it. To differentiate true courage from the humbuggery and the lunatic fringe aping it, it is necessary to stress the eminently *rational* character of the virtue, and to point out that it has eyes as well as fists. Otherwise, the noble virtue would come under the odium rightly attached to the antics of the semi-lunatic who flirts with death on the steeple of a lofty building to thrill a morbid crowd and to satisfy his own pathological vanity.

My friend, the genial scholar, William Lyon Phelps, cites Robert Clive who later became Lord Clive, and is generally known as Clive of India, as probably the most courageous man he has ever read about. The facts which he instances, however, seem to display for the most part such an utter recklessness that I find it difficult to regard him as a man of true courage, a man who undertakes risks only for justifying reasons.

On two occasions, Clive pointed a loaded revolver at his temple and pulled the trigger, only to have the gun jam. On another occasion, inexperienced in shooting, he accused a captain of cheating and challenged him to a gun duel and missed. The captain then could have killed him. Is it prudent or rational or wise for a person inexperienced with a gun to challenge a veteran expert? It may be reckless; it may be a piece of daredeviltry. But enlightened courage? Scarcely.

After the captain had Clive at his mercy, he asked:

"Did I cheat?"

"Go to hell," answered Clive.

Was this courage or reckless bravado? Just what was to be gained by further antagonizing the man who had it in his power to finish off the unsuccessful duelist? Perhaps an emotional release, perhaps a bit of exhibitionism, but of values worthwhile—and human life is such a value—none. For some reason not mentioned, the captain forewent his privilege of finishing his opponent off—but no thanks to Clive that he did.

In his conquest of India, many of the risks Clive underwent were probably for considerations of proportionate gravity. Before reaching fifty, Clive passed out of the picture—a suicide. This is distinctly a piece of cowardice: it always requires more courage to live and face difficulties than to escape by turning the cannon of destruction upon oneself and slinking off in ignominy. From what Professor Phelps relates of Clive, I would rate him a daredevil, a reckless man, but not one of enlightened courage. And if there is no light in courage, is it courage at all?

Cheerfulness Inherent in Courage

Life is filled with occasions which challenge our courage and our fortitude. Courage is not confined to the doing of the spectacular and the unusual. Courage of a high order is required to face the daily grind and do it not grudgingly, but cheerfully and well. The prosaic and homely tasks which face the father in earning a living for his family, the menial duties which dog mother's footsteps from sun-up to sunset in caring for her brood, call for genuine courage to fulfill them with joyous serenity.

The note of cheerfulness is inherent in courage. It demands that a difficult and often painful duty not only be done, but be done cheerfully. Whining, petulance, sourness stain and begrime the splendor of a difficult deed and strip it of the shining radiance of cheerful willingness—the authentic mark of true courage. How many there are who have spoiled many a good deed and robbed it of its radiance by complaining about it, either before they did it or afterwards. If they could only have suppressed the whine and the sour look, how vastly more appealing the deed, how much greater the upwelling of gratitude to them. The deed then would have the smiling face of courage. Perhaps that is why Barrie is fond of calling courage "the lovely virtue," and speaks of it in his own beautiful way as "the rib of Himself that God sent down to His children." Certain it is that courage has in the core of its being a cheerfulness that transmutes a dull, monotonous or dangerous task into one of quiet joy and serenity.

"A true knight," observes Sir Philip Sidney, "is full of gay bravery in the midst of danger." Similar is the observation of Emerson: "And that which takes my fancy most in the heroic class is the good humor and hilarity they exhibit."

We think of the Christian martyrs facing the swordsman not with frowns or groanings or complaints, but with smiles of joy mantling their countenances, happy that they were counted worthy of the martyr's crown. Indeed, we frequently find them pleading for the honor and the joy of sealing their faith in the Crucified with their life's blood. Thus, St. Peter, welcoming the cross, requested only that he be crucified head downward, not being worthy, as he said, to be crucified in the manner of his Lord.

Courage, then, is the magic alchemy which transmutes not only a dull and monotonous task but even an excruciating ordeal into a labor of cheerfulness and joy.

A Divine Ally

Not less than seven times in the Old Testament do we find the admonition: "Be of good courage." In the Second

Book of Kings, Joab says: "Be of good courage, and let us fight for our people, and for the city of our God; and the Lord will do what is good in His sight." In this utterance there is the implied confidence that if Joab and his people fight with courage for the city of God, and do their best, the Lord will be their invisible ally and they cannot fail. This, too, is the meaning underlying Lincoln's noble declaration: "God and one constitute a majority."

The Psalmist likewise expresses the conviction that divine aid will not be lacking the man of courage who places his trust in God. "Wait on the Lord." he counsels, "be of good courage, and He shall strengthen thine heart." It is this inner confidence that God is at his side which brings a smile to the man of courage and bids him be of good cheer. With God on my side, he asks, who is there who can hurt me? Who is there who can rob me of ultimate victory? Thus re-enforced with a divine Ally, he goes out to face danger with a smile and "greets the unseen with a cheer." This is the note which St. Teresa sounds in her famous book-mark, which will richly repay memorizing:

Let naught disturb thee,
Naught fright thee ever,
All things are passing,
God changeth never.
Patience e'er conquers;
With God for thine own
Thou nothing dost lack—
He sufficeth alone.

What the sun is to vegetative life, God is to courage in

the hearts of men. Place a board upon the verdant grass reaching up eagerly after the winter's snows for the kiss of spring's sunshine. In a short time it will wither and die, for the sun is the source of its energy and sustaining vitality. Remove God from the minds of men and the wellspring of their courage and joyous serenity will speedily dry up.

When men are subjected to long suffering and their stamina is being tested to the limit, it is noteworthy that, even if unaccustomed to pray, they turn instinctively to God for courage and strength like blades of withered grass reaching desperately for the sun. "There are no atheists," declared General MacArthur, "in the foxholes of Bataan." In times of ease and indulgence, men may forget God. In times of crises and ordeal, they turn to Him for strength to endure, to dare, to fight through to victory.

In our study of courage and methods of developing it, we shall treat of fear and show how it can be restrained, directed and made to serve a useful purpose. While anxiety and unfounded fears are to be removed as obstacles to the growth of courage, some fear in the presence of danger is natural, healthy and is not the opposite of courage. Both fear and courage may fill the same breast at the same time. "True courage," says the National Research Council, "is the ability to act as you believe you should in the face of recognized danger—to act in spite of fear—to risk your life to keep the soldier's faith."

Anxiety, however, is the enemy of courage. Fear is a reaction proportionate to the danger confronting a person. Anxiety is a disproportionate reaction to danger, or even a reaction to imaginary danger. It is fear which has exceeded its bounds of usefulness and becomes a dynamic center of neuroses and ultimately leads to complexes which thwart and strangle the emotional and mental life.

Biotonic Function

The function of fear is twofold. The first is biotonic—the arousal of the greatest potency of the resources of the organism toward the avoidance of danger. This is accomplished by the action of the sympathetic nervous system upon some of the glands which are stimulated to secrete abundantly of substances which activate the muscles and the nervous system, while they arrest other functions such as nutrition and reproduction. Fear stimulates the secretion of the thyroid gland which is so essential for the rapid functioning of the living cell.

Fear likewise quickens the secretion of the adrenal gland, which constricts the blood supply to the vegetative organs in the abdomen, while it dilates the blood vessels which go to the voluntary muscles and the nervous system as well as to the lungs and the heart. Adrenalin, which is nature's own "shot in the arm," causes the sugars to be released into the blood stream to serve as fuel for the human fighting machine. The heart beats faster, pumping blood more rapidly to the arms, legs and brain, where its oxygen is needed. The lungs respond to the alarm signal with quickened breathing.

Blood pressure goes up; there occur subtle changes in body chemistry, automatically effected by powerful emotion, which protect a person in action in ways he would never think of, if he had to figure them out himself. His blood clots more quickly. For the time being, he loses the sense of fatigue even though he may have been dog tired. He experiences a sense of vigor, feels the thrill of overcoming danger and stirs with the zest of combat. Thus does fear mobilize all the latent resources of a person to meet a danger and to deal with it effectively.

Educational Function

The second function of fear is educational. By alerting man to the danger, fear arouses him to circumvent the peril and hence stimulates his intelligence and develops his intellectual interests. The most powerful stimulant to foresight is fear; it is therefore the mother of prudence and of enlightened courage; it plays an enormous part in man's survival. It is the prudent who survive and the foolhardy who perish. There is a world of difference between prudent courage and daredeviltry. "Fools rush in where angels fear to tread." Whittier expresses it thus:

> *Not to him who rashly dares;*
> *But to him who nobly bears,*
> *Is the victor's garland sure.*

It is evident, therefore, that the development of courage does not entail the ignoring of danger signals nor the lessening of the sense of prudent fear. These are the foundations of enlightened courage, courage with eyes—the only courage which is conducive to the success and happiness of a person. Disproportionate fears, unfounded fears, unreasonable fears, shadow fears which are stubborn survivals of dangers no longer extant and all the brood of anxieties which are born of imaginary perils and excessive fears are of course to be eradicated.

Psychiatry has penetrated deeply into the treatment of fear and anxiety, but had done comparatively little in the study of courage. We shall avail ourselves of the findings of psychiatry for the conquest of unreasonable apprehensions and shall present considerations and methods for the development of courage. We shall lean heavily upon incidents to illustrate our principles and methods and to take the discussion from the theoretical and the abstract to the concrete and the practical, where the greatest help can be rendered.

Summary

*Remember then, you—the student, the grocer, the clerk, the housewife, the businessman—*can *develop the habit of courage. You can do this by weighing the risks against the advantages, the dangers against the returns, and then acting with despatch and determination. Reflect upon the values which you will achieve and you will find your will strengthened and your determination increased. Courage flows from the clear perception of a worthwhile end which transcends your immediate petty interests and advances those long-range values in which your deepest welfare and true happiness lie. Acquire the habit of doing cheerfully and resolutely that which your judgment tells you is the wisest and the best and soon you will have the habit so deeply grooved as to do it quickly and with ease.*

RULE 1. *Form the habit of deciding what things are worth while and set yourself to achieve them in spite of difficulties and hardships and thus you will acquire the habit of enlightened courage.*

Reflect upon the instances of courage cited in this chapter and wait until tomorrow to read the next.

CHAPTER TWO

COURAGE UNDER FIRE

You cannot choose your battlefield
The gods do that for you,
But you can plant a standard
Where a standard never flew.

—Nathalia Crane, *The Colors*

AN IMPORTANT STEP *in the development of courage is the realization that in struggling for a righteous cause one has a divine Ally. Human nature shrinks almost instinctively from loneliness and yearns for comradeship. The National Research Council reports that a tremendous boost to morale results when the roll call is taken in a company of hard-pressed soldiers. It helps each one realize that he is not fighting alone. It makes him keenly conscious of the strength that comes from united effort. It revives his waning spirits and fills him with new courage and determination to fight through to victory.*

Even more powerful in bolstering one's spirits is the consciousness that one has God on his side and can turn to Him for help and strength when the odds are piled high against him. Prayer is the means of tapping divine power. No one has ever lifted his mind and heart to God in a cry for aid without receiving strength and courage. When an individual has done his best and finds himself at the end of his resources, he turns to God and thereby derives new power and fresh determination. This is one of the important steps in the development of courage which we shall illustrate in this chapter.

Three Kinds

We may deepen our insight into the nature of courage by examining its various forms and the circumstances which surround their manifestations. There are three kinds of courage, namely, physical, intellectual, and moral. It is not always possible to isolate them, as they frequently overlap. A single achievement may involve all three. Nevertheless, it is often possible to put the proper label upon the dominant quality. Thus, athletic sports afford opportunities for the display of physical gameness. So, likewise, do martial enterprises and all other forms of physical combat.

Under this heading would fall also exhibitions of fortitude and stamina such as shipwrecked sailors and aviators have given in rafts and on planks for many weeks in the open sea. The country has been stirred by new sagas of the sea written in the tortured endurance of men whose staying power seemed to know no limit.

One story, which Captain Eddie Rickenbacker tells with such modesty and restraint, pictures eight men suddenly catapulted into a rough sea. For twenty-one days they floated in their three small rafts, with the sun baking them by day and the cold winds freezing them at night. They were tortured with a constant thirst, only slightly allayed by a little rain water squeezed out of their rotting clothes.

They were weakened by a gnawing hunger, only occasionally allayed by a sea gull or a raw fish. Unable to stretch their limbs because of their cramped quarters, their bodies pained them incessantly and sleep came to them but intermittently and briefly.

"I would sometimes come out of nightmare," relates Rickenbaker, "and pull in the tow lines until they fetched up hard, and I knew the others were still there. Other times, I would hear moans or groans, or a cry and often a prayer. Or I would see a shadow move and twist as a man tried to ease his torture."

Turn to God

Sharks followed them and repeatedly struck the bottom of their rubber rafts, waiting impatiently for the kill. The back of the oldest member, Colonel Adamson, had been injured in the landing on the sea, and every wave that hit the raft, every shark that lunged against the bottom, made him feel "as if some one is kicking me in the kidneys." The burning thirst made Sergeant Alex delirious and caused him to gulp the salt water in a futile effort to ease the conflagration within him.

On the evening of the tenth day, Alex was growing weaker. Rickenbacker had him transferred to his boat. "I put my arm around him," he related, "as a mother cuddles a child, hoping in that way to transfer the heat of my body to him during the night. In an hour or so his shivering stopped and sleep came—a shallow sleep in which Alex mumbled intermittently in Polish, phrases about his mother and his girl 'Snooks.' " Two days later, he died. For another eight days the men held on grimly, though they were now like living skeletons.

During those long days and unending nights the men, some of whom had not prayed for years, kept their hope and their courage alive by prayer, the singing of hymns and the reading of the New Testament. With death staring them in the face, their thoughts turned to God and they clung to Him in prayer. Rickenbacker relates that one day, about an hour after he had ended his prayer, a gull suddenly lighted on his head. Its body, divided among the crew, tided them over a period when death from sheer starvation and weakness seemed imminent.

A passage from the New Testament that they never failed to read aloud each evening was: "Be not solicitous therefore, saying, What shall we eat; or what shall we drink, and wherewith shall we be clothed? . . . For your Father knoweth that you have need of all these things. Seek ye therefore first the kingdom of God, and His justice, and all these things shall be added unto you. Be not therefore solicitous for tomorrow, for the morrow will be solititous for itself. Sufficient for the day is the evil thereof."

The testimony of all these members of different faiths and of different habits of life shows how men turn almost instinctively to God when their backs are against the wall and they are at the end of the tether of their own resources. From the divine Source they derive strength and courage to carry on when all human aid is beyond their reach.

Naked Courage vs. the Sea

Not less remarkable was the fortitude, the pluck and courage displayed by Dixon, Pastula and Aldrich, the crew of a bomber which became lost on the South Pacific. For thirty-four days they floated in their tiny rubber raft, enduring indescribable tortures of thirst and hunger, burning by day and freezing by night. Long after being given up for dead, they turned up on a nameless island, to which they had to fight their way through a heavy sea. Let us compare their achievement with that of Captain Bligh, which has been for so many years the classic of the sea.

The famous Englishman, with his seventeen men from the *Bounty,* sailed from Tofua in the South Pacific to Tiemor, Netherlands East Indies, a distance of 3,618 miles, in forty-eight days. But Bligh had a 23-foot boat, 32 pounds of pork, 150 pounds of bread, 28 gallons of water, 6 quarts of rum, 6 bottles of wine, a quadrant, a compass and canvas. In contrast with such equipment, Dixon and his two companions had a pocket knife, a pair of pliers, an automatic pistol, that was soon rendered useless by rust, and a length of line. They were without food or water. They had no instruments, no means of controlling their inflated raft.

Nevertheless, Dixon contrived a series of ingenious make-shifts by which he charted his course and controlled his craft. They used their rotting clothing to catch rain and speared a few fish—not enough, however, for one good meal. The raft capsized so easily that they lost what little they had, including the last pieces of clothing. Here they were with nothing, without even a stitch of clothing to protect them from the blistering equatorial sun. Nothing but naked hands and youthful gameness with which to fight the shoreless sea, the squalls, and the elements.

Their plight toward the last was desperate in the extreme. On the thirty-third day their raft was capsized by a huge breaker, and they were so exhausted that they had barely strength enough to right the raft and drag themselves panting upon it.

"Each Evening They Prayed"

Was there to be no end to this terrific beating they were taking? Hunger was devouring them; thirst was choking them; the sun was scalding their mist-drenched, naked bodies. The sea was pummeling them, tossing their raft upside down, till they were groggy. Thoughts of ending their torture by sliding over the raft into the all-embracing arms of the angry sea came to them.

They had prayed day after day to God, and with His help managed to drive such temptations away. Chief petty officer Dixon relates that, though he had not darkened a church door for sixteen years, he found himself turning constantly to God in his desperate plight. Each evening they prayed and sang hymns together and found their faith and courage renewed. Like Rickenbacker and his companions, they, too, learned in the fiery furnace of suffering the truth of Tennyson's lines:

More things are wrought by prayer
Than this world dreams of.

When their minds cleared and their panting ceased, they buckled up their courage for the *nth* time.

"We've come thus far," said Tony Pastula, "and by God we'll go on!"

They shook hands all around, and vowed to go on.

That night, showers beat an angry tattoo upon their naked bodies. Each drop felt like an icy bullet as it hit their feverish, sun-baked flesh. They scooped up the water with their hands, and then huddled together for warmth.

The next morning they spied a huge black shark, weighing upwards of a thousand pounds, following them a few yards away. He was getting impatient for his breakfast, too long delayed.

On the thirty-fourth day they sighted a little island, and with their hands rowed feverishly toward it. Murderous breakers were beating the coral reef ahead of them. When at last they were hurled into the churning waters, and dragged themselves to the shore, they were so exhausted that they could not stand. It was a great saga of the sea they wrote, an epic in fortitude, pluck against hopeless odds, and a perseverance that knew no ending.

Their long struggle with the elements shows what human nature can endure when the heart of courage pumps the life-sustaining blood of pluck and gameness through the veins. If their morale had crumpled under the beating of the elements, the taut thread of life, often at the breaking point, would doubtless have snapped long before. Their experience and that of scores of others whose long ordeals in open life boats have come to our attention, show that men do not live by bread alone, but by pluck and courage, when all the odds are against them. Naked and empty-handed, they proved the truth of Thomas Fuller's observation: "A man of courage never wants weapons."

A New Record

Before me, as I write these lines, is a picture showing my friend, Chaplain Robert D. White, standing with U. S. Seaman Bernard Izzi before a crucifix. Izzi is uttering a prayer of gratitude for his rescue *after eighty-three days adrift in the open sea*—a new record of human endurance.

After his vessel was sunk by enemy torpedoes November 2, 1943, about 300 miles off the Atlantic coast of South America, Izzi clung to wreckage for two days and two nights before he was picked up by four sailors on a life raft. They made their meager provisions stretch out for twenty-five days. "Then," relates Izzi, "we were really up against it."

At night, gulls would occasionally light on their raft, and Izzi and his companions would catch as many as they could and eat them raw. They also managed to catch some fish with their hands and with a pair of scissors fastened to a stick. The scissors soon broke, however.

Dangling their toes in the water to lure some small sharks closer, they caught several, some with an improvised noose, and some with their bare hands. They ate them raw. On the sixtieth day, Seaman Beasley died. Ensign Maddox held out till the seventy-seventh day. Izzi and two Dutch seamen were left.

It is interesting to note that the three survivors, fighting with their backs to the wall, turned to God for aid in their dire extremity. Of different faiths and different languages, they spoke the universal Esperanto of prayer—the language to which practically all men turn in great emergencies.

"We would go for days without water," young Izzi related, "and all we could do was to pray for rain. About a week before we were picked up, we went without any water for six days. It was terrible.

"We prayed all day and all night during those six days. I couldn't remember very many prayers, but I just kept saying the Our Father, the Hail Mary and the Apostle's Creed over and over again, and kept pleading with God to help us. The two Dutch sailors who were with me prayed hard, too. But I just knew our prayers were going to be answered.

"One night, we had prayed harder than ever. Our prayers were answered the next day when it rained plenty and the going really got rough. But we got plenty of water."

On January 24 they were picked up by a convoy and brought to Brazil. Normally weighing 145 pounds, Izzi had wasted away to eighty. Like his two companions, he had shrunk to skin and bones. They all agreed that their prayers had buoyed them up when the going was the toughest and had given them the confidence and the heart to fight to the bitter end. The incident shows once again how faith and prayer tap a well-spring of divine strength, and from a divine Ally there comes the courage that snatches victory from the jaws of death.

Courage Releases New Energy

The survival of these and other shipwrecked mariners after long ordeals with the sea and the elements reveals the existence of latent stores of energy which are seldom tapped in ordinary living. Courage is the auger which bores through to these deep resources. If courage is lacking, these ulterior powers are not reached and the resistance goes sputtering out after a half-hearted effort.

If one can banish fear or even lessen its undue opression and paralysis, one secures a new release of energy and determination. About a dozen years ago, I learned of an incident related by a survivor of the *Morro Castle,* which went down in flames off the New Jersey coast.

"The few inadequate life boats had been lowered," he said, "and the flames were spreading like wildfire through the ship. Panic and terror gripped the remaining passengers. Desperate, I jumped overboard.

"Floundering about in the water, I looked up. One scene is etched indelibly in my memory.

"Poised on the deck was a young red-haired girl who had donned a bathing suit. She was about to dive when suddenly she spied me directly below. She stopped and called:

" 'Do you think we'll make it, big boy? Let's show them we can.'

"Then, with a smile and a wave of the hand, she dove into the sea. The waves were high, and I didn't see her after that.

"I don't know whether she made it or not. But if she did, I would like her to know that it was her smile in the face of death that loosened something within me and nerved me for the long swim to the Jersey coast ten miles away."

I suppose it is only youth that could laugh with such light-heartedness in the face of such overwhelming odds. There is a buoyancy, a gaiety, a venturesomeness which is distinctive of youth. The buoyancy and the lightheartedness may bog down with the years, and bid farewell, but courage goes all the way. A smile in the face of danger, a courageous gesture under fire, on the part of young or old, pulls the trigger of latent energy necessary to reach the goal.

While by no means confined to youth, the craving for adventure is doubtless more intense in youth. When war threatens the life and limb of every combatant, do young men seek positions of comparative safety? By and large, they seek to enlist in services such as the air corps, which will bring them into the thick of it. They want to fill their quivering nostrils with the fiery breath of combat high in the shining skies where the playing is "for keeps."

During the war years my classes at Notre Dame were thinned down week after week. When I bade "Goodbye" to a student leaving for the service, I seem to recall him saying most frequently: "Goodbye, Father, I'm off for the Air Corps." "I'm off for the Marines." "I'm off for the torpedo squadron." Truly, the spirit of venture, of combat, is deep in the heart of youth.

Daring of Commandos

Youthful courage and daring found their crystallization in a unique organization of the war—the Commandos.

Tough, well-disciplined, quick-thinking and hard-hitting, they undertook the most hazardous of all assignments. The chances of a rendezvous with death were always high, yet there was no dearth of volunteers.

One of the most daring undertakings of this or any war was the attempt of the Commandos to get General Erwin Rommel, dead or alive. General Sir Claude Auchenleck was convinced that if Rommel were captured or killed, the striking power of the Axis forces would crumble. Such was the hair-raising mission assigned the Commandos.

Two groups of fifty were crammed into two submarines that slipped from their moorings at Alexandria, Egypt, at dusk on November 14, 1941. The expedition was under the command of twenty-four-year-old Geoffrey Keyes, youngest lieutenant-colonel in the British army. Because of mechanical difficulties, one of the submarines was obliged to turn back; the other continued and the next evening pulled in close to the shore east of Tobruk. Wearing black coveralls and sneakers, their faces blackened, the fifty Commandos went ashore in collapsible rubber boats; twenty remained to guard the boats, the others started their trek across the desert to Rommel's headquarters, a large villa in the midst of a German encampment at Sidi Raffa.

For two days the thirty Commandos lay hidden in a dried-up river bed, covered with sand. During the night they stretched their legs and ate their meager rations. Under the cover of darkness on the 17th they threaded their way toward Rommel's villa. They carried revolvers, Tommy guns, Bren guns and hand grenades. Upon reaching the villa, the Commandos politely knocked on the front door, and garrotted the German sentry, who opened it, before he could make on outcry. While a number remained outside to fight off Nazi reinforcements, Keyes and the others hurried down the ground-floor hall in search of Rommel.

Asking no quarter and giving none, the Commandos kicked open doors and sprayed the room with their automatic guns blazing away. In one room they startled Nazi staff officers working late over their maps, and mowed them down before they could reach for a gun. Nazi guards, who came running down the stairs to investigate the shooting, met a similar fate.

Cool-headed Execution

Kicking open another door, Keyes stepped across the threshold. A burst of machine-gun fire tore open his stomach and killed him instantly. Right behind him was Captain Robin Campbell. Quickly pulling his leader's body back into the hall, he flung two hand grenades into the room, blowing it into pieces.

The entire German camp had now been aroused. At the front door the Commandos were blazing away furiously at the swarming Nazi reinforcements. Young Campbell now took command outside. He blew his whistle for his followers to assemble around him. Only eight of the thirty responded.

They were loathe to leave, however, without making one further desperate effort to get Rommel. They hurled grenades into the upstairs windows of the villa, hoping to blast Rommel in his bedroom. Captain Campbell's leg was shattered by a Nazi bullet, and he slumped to the ground. Handing his last two grenades to his comrades, he said:

"Blow up the powder plant, and then leave me behind."

They were reluctant to leave him, but he commanded them to do so, as he was unwilling to burden them. Giving him a quick shot of morphine, they propped him up against a tree and fled. Making an incredible escape from the Nazi camp, they reached the beach, only to find their comrades had been attacked and their rubber boats destroyed. Fleeing back into the desert, they hoped to hold out until they could reach British forces, but most of them ran into Axis patrols which were now scouring that area intensively. Only two of the original fifty made their way to the British lines, forty-one days later. Their brave attempt to get Rommel failed, because he was in Rome that night. They wrought untold damage to staff headquarters, however, and wrote a new epic of courage and daring in the blood-stained annals of war.

It was not a mere piece of reckless daredeviltry, but of daredeviltry lit up with imagination, intelligence, careful planning and cool-headed execution. True, they failed in their main objective. It is not in the power of mortals to command success; they can only deserve it.

Summary

In addition to the prayers which the Commandos undoubtedly said, they identified themselves with a cause which transcended their petty interests, their safety and even their lives. Such identification is closely akin to prayer and never fails to tap new sources of power and energy.

Much of the fear and anxiety paralyzing so many individuals today is traceable to their absorption with themselves. They are so concerned with their petty aches and pains that they make themselves the center of the universe, the focal point of all their striving. Such self-centered egotism constitutes the fertile breeding grounds for a host of engrossing cares, phobias and anxieties which dim the vision, dwarf the enthusiasm and paralyze the motor nerves of their unhappy victims.

The remedy is decentralization: a proper perspective must be achieved. One's own safety must be seen as of little consequence when compared with such great causes as the defense of human liberty and the safety of one's country. Such a perspective inspired not only Nathan Hale but also other uncounted patriots to lament that they had but one life to give for their country.

"Persons who become concerned with the welfare of other people," points out the psychiatrist, Dr. T. A. Williams, "soon shed needless fear. Thus the parasitic woman shielded from any real trouble, who is afraid to venture alone in the streets of a large city because her imagination clothes them with a dread of assault, may be contrasted with the missionary, the professional welfare worker, the district nurse and the newspaper woman who travel unconcerned into districts which are viewed with horror by the former. The remedy, of course, is the realization that one's own part in the great scheme of things is not of transcendent importance, and that to fulfill one's obligations is a greater thing than to avoid pain."

Turning to God in prayer and the identification of one's self with a cause of transcendent value are, then, important steps in the conquest of fear and in the attainment of that high courage which lies behind every achievement of surpassing worth.

RULE 2. *Identify yourself with a noble cause, far bigger than yourself and your petty interests, and turn often to God in prayer for help to carry on, and you will find courage flooding your soul.*

Reflect upon the instances of courage cited in this chapter and wait until tomorrow to read the next chapter.

Chapter Three

THE GRIDIRON OF COURAGE

A stout heart breaks bad luck.

—Cervantes, *Don Quixote*

Acting courageously is subject to the laws of habit formation. The best way to develop an act into a habit is to perform it frequently: repetition grooves the act into the nervous system and tends to make the reaction to a similar situation habitual. Fortunate indeed is the individual who early in life has learned to face a disturbing situation, analyze the elements of danger, weigh the pros and cons, and who then, having made his decision, acts with calmness, vigor and courage. When that is done frequently, that manner of reacting becomes habitual and courage becomes a constituent element in the habit.

How can such situations be created for youth? Competitive sports provide the answer. They offer difficulty, hardship, and the ever-present danger of defeat, without serious threat to life or limb. They demand that the participants confront the opposition, analyze its points of strength and weakness, and then mobilize their resources in the whole-hearted and determined effort to outmaneuver and outsmart the enemy. These are the habits which are essential to the achievement of success in all the enterprises of life.

One reason why competitive sports have taken such a hold on the American public and are encouraged in all our schools is because of the realization that they contribute a valuable supplement to the work with books by developing habits of resourcefulness, discipline and courage. Along with the ideals, these habits constitute the basis of character; the building of manly, wholesome character is one of the chief ends of education.

Participation in all forms of competitive sport is calculated to develop the important habits of initiative, patience and courage which are essential to success in all the enterprises of life. In this chapter we shall cite instances from the field of intercollegiate sports to show how such habits are developed and how those habits can subsequently be utilized to good advantage for the welfare of the individual and of society.

Moral Equivalent of War

No matter how cultured or civilized society may become, it can ill afford to dispense with the basic instinct of combativeness, the elemental endowment of pugnacity. This deeply rooted instinct in man has been responsible in no small degree for the qualities of fortitude, stamina, resourcefulness, tenacity, grit and courage. Without these, no society would grow strong or long endure. These qualities are developed in a superb degree in war, but the cost is too high.

The great problem facing society, then, is the development of a moral equivalent of war. This was the thesis which William James developed around the turn of the century; the validity of his contention is, I think, beyond question. The combative virtues mentioned must be retained and developed, but without the frightful destruction which war always entails; otherwise, Mars will destroy our civilization and kill off the race.

Competitive sports have been found to serve as at least a part of the moral equivalent of war. They develop the fighting spirit; they place a premium upon grit, resourcefulness, courage. They stimulate the pugnacious instinct; they channel its expression, however, into socially wholesome conduct. Competitive athletics seeks to groove the combative instinct into the building of strong character which will fight with courage and insight for the social good. Accustomed to opposition on the playing field, such a character will not crumble before organized resistance in the fields of social endeavor and civic enterprise.

Competitive sports develop the capacity to think quickly, to analyze the offense with lightning discernment, to mobilize instantly all one's physical and mental resources and fling them wholeheartedly into the fray. They place a premium upon pluck, will power, cool-headedness, courage, daring, and the refusal to admit defeat till the last whistle has sounded. They inculcate the sportsmanship of losing without an alibi and of winning without boasting.

Turning Defeat into Victory

As our primary interest is in the study of courage and, as these qualities all cluster around that central core, we think it will be worth while to turn our gaze for a few minutes upon the playing field to see how courage has asserted itself and what victories it has plucked from the very jaws of defeat.

No campus has a monopoly on courage. In the annals of every school, large or small, are recorded deeds of lion-hearted players whose pluck and daring turned the bitter pill of defeat into the sweet morsel of victory. The alumni of every school are fond of reminiscencing over the feats of their Eckersals, Thorpes, Nevers, Cagles, Granges, Gipps and Harmons. The feats of their fighting heroes play no unimportant roles in the building of the traditions which form the soul or spirit of a school. True, the notes they sound are marginal. Not infrequently, however, they become the overtones which give the orchestration of the school's spirit its distinctive tone and melody.

While athletics must always be kept subordinate to the principal purposes for which institutions of learning exist, they have rightly come to be regarded as inescapably necessary activities of channeling into socially useful habits the superabundant energy and ebullience of youth. Dam up that outlet and try to direct all the streams of youthful energy into the solitary channel of intellectual effort. You find that it can't be done; the stream of energy is too wide and strong and torrential to be cramped, cabined, and confined into such narrow straits. It floods over the banks into destructive inundations of the social landscape.

As all my life has been spent on the campuses of universities—Illinois, Oxford and Notre Dame—I find it easy and pleasant to recall instances of pluck and courage at these and other institutions as well. I will try to confine myself to citing just a few typical examples. The instances I shall cite are drawn from the campus of my Alma Mater, the University of Illinois, and from that of Notre Dame, my present home. Students of other schools will see in them, I'm sure, but mirrors which reflect many such scenes upon the playing fields of their own campuses. It is in that humble spirit that I instance them.

"A Fighting Heart"

Of the many cases of pluck and courage that throng back to me from the Illinois campus, I will cite as typical that of one of my students, Harold E. Kenney. A wrestler of unusual promise, Harold was involved in a serious auto accident that threatened to render him an invalid for life. Instead of simply bewailing his sad fortune, Harold went through long hours of exercise daily. He brought back life and vigor to arms and legs that threatened to be useless. Out of a badly shattered and broken body he built one so strong that he withstood the onslaughts of the best welterweight wrestlers of the Big Ten and ended by winning the Conference crown. It was an inspiring display of what will power, pluck and grit can accomplish in the face of enormous handicaps.

"What is not less necessary than size and physical strength," I often heard Coach Bob Zuppke remark, "is a fighting heart. When that is lacking, nothing will take its place." He inculcated a spirit of fighting courage into his players which earned for them, in good seasons and in bad, the soubriquet, "The Fighting Illini."

In years gone by, I listened to many a discussion between football fans as to the comparative greatness of those two immortals of the gridiron—"Red" Grange and George Gipp. It was never my good fortune to see the great Gipp in action, but I did see every game that Grange played on the home field in his three years as an All-American. While I can't compare him with the stars of other days, whom I never saw, Grange is the most brilliant halfback whom I have seen tote a ball over a period of more than thirty years.

On an October day in 1924, I was seated with a little group of men who were dedicating the newly erected Illinois Memorial Stadium. I had been chairman of the Champaign Township organization in the state-wide drive for funds for its erection. Among the number on the platform was Coach Yost, whose team was soon to face Grange and his mates. Yost wanted to size up this new star in the football firmament, who had such an uncanny knack of catching the kick-off and running for a touchdown. When asked if he thought Grange would duplicate such a feat against Michigan, Yost was quoted in a local paper as saying he would take off the field any team of his which permitted such a feat. Whether the quotation be accurate or not, one can be sure that his players were well trained by this wily strategist, who ranks with the great coaches of all time, in forming a defense against such an open-field runner.

A "Galloping Ghost"

In the game against Michigan, they fearlessly kicked off to Grange. He caught the ball on his four yard line and raced like a meteor through the entire team all the way for a touchdown! Three more times in the first half he raced over for touchdowns. Most of them were long runs. I don't think I shall ever again have such a sensation of stunned amazement and rapturous surprise as I did on that unforgettable October afternoon.

Back of those scintillating performances which thrilled spectators throughout the country and lifted this sophomore into national fame and placed him as an overwhelming favorite on every All-American selection is the story of unsurpassed gameness and of a fighting heart. He was all that Zuppke had ever asked for in this last quality. True, he had speed and a marvelous deception, but this would have availed him little, if he did not have that lion-hearted courage of never regarding himself stopped or tackled. Time after time he would be hit hard and knocked almost to the ground, only to retain his footing and carry on. Time after time he wriggled and squirmed out of the arms of a swarm of eager tacklers. I have seen him carrying on after being hit half a dozen times, so that he was actually groggy. Still his fighting heart and his unconquerable combative instinct drove him on. He was that unusual blend of amazing speed, bewildering deception and a fighting heart which occurs just about once in a decade. It won him the name of the "Galloping Ghost" of football, and I doubt if my eyes will ever look upon his like again.

The quality which won him a unique niche in the hearts of the student body was the modesty which like a crown of lustrous jewels sat upon his gridiron greatness. Modest and retiring as any second stringer on the team, I never heard him boast or brag; he gave the credit for his phenomenal success to the craftiness of his coach and the team work of his mates. His football suit with its famous numeral 77 is hung in Illinois' Hall of Fame, and gallops no more across the striped greens of the Middle West. But the epic of a fighting heart and the sage of a courage that never knew defeat are among the proud traditions and the treasured heritages of Illinois.

The Notre Dame Tradition

What Vienna is to music, Paris to art, London to empire, New York to finance, Hollywood to the movies, Notre Dame is to football. Year after year her team travels from coast to coast to take on all comers, and usually emerges high in the list of the season's greatest elevens. The courage and the daring which Notre Dame teams traditionally display have won for her millions of synthetic alumni who have never seen the campus, but who adopt her team as their own and identify themselves with her fortunes on the striped green.

"In the landings at Salerno in which both British and Americans participated," wrote an American soldier, "someone started to sing, and the song was picked up all along the line. The song the British sang, the song the Americans sang, as they went through the hell of Salerno, wasn't *The Star Spangled Banner.* It wasn't *God Save the King.* It was *Cheer, Cheer for Old Notre Dame.*"

The tradition of an invincible will to win and of gameness under fire cluster around the immortal Knute Rockne, who brought such magic, wizardy, and dramatic appeal to the gridirons of the nation. His name is synonymous with courage that has both eyes and hands. "When the going gets tough," he used to say, "is when we really begin to fight." Against the strongest teams in the country he was accustomed to start his second stringers, whom he affectionately called his "ponies."

When they would be lined up against a team that towered above them in size and weight, he would remind them: "The bigger they are, the harder they fall." In line with this, he pitted his 155-pound Johnny Metzger against the colossal guards of the nation and usually saw him outcharge, outsmart and outmaneuver them. Stories of Metzger's incredible feats preceded him and usually brought expressions of disdain from his prospective adversaries, only to have it change into chagrin when the tiny piece of dynamite began to explode before them. Rockne's lines were generally much lighter than those of his opponents, but they made up for their lack of weight with an abundance of speed and fight.

George Gipp Writes History

When asked to name his all-time team, Rockne would shy from answering. Either he did not wish to enter into invidious comparisons and hurt the feeling of his former stars, or he never got around to selecting the best eleven out of the myriads whom he developed. But his intimates did reveal that he had a unique admiration tinged with affection for George Gipp, his famous fullback. The feats of the "Gipper" have become legendary among the followers of the Fighting Irish. I find on the campus of Notre Dame much the same stirrings of admiration and idolatry which obtained at Illinois for their immortal Grange.

"Who was the greater of the two?" I've often asked the old timers when they return to Notre Dame. I have yet to find the follower of the Irish who would concede any superior within his era to the redoubtable "Gipper," who could run and pass and kick with the best of the specialists in all these lines. So outstanding was Gipp that Rockne knew he would not cause any hard feelings among any of his all-time "greats" by characterizing Gipp as "the greatest player Notre Dame ever developed. He was unequalled in the game by anybody, save, perhaps, Jim Thorpe."

Six-foot-two, weighing 185 pounds, George was a splendid blend of speed, deception, and resourcefulness. As an instance of the latter, Rockne often related an incident in the game against the Army in 1919.

The cadets had a slight lead. But Notre Dame came back with a passing attack that culminated with a bullet-like shot from Gipp to Bahan on the Army's one-yard line. The teams had lined up and Larson, at center, was waiting for the quarterback to start calling signals. Suddenly, Gipp called sharply:

"Pass me the ball."

Catching it while the players of both teams stood frozen in their tracks, he dove over for a touchdown. It was none too soon, for, just as the ball touched Gipp's fingers, the official sounded his horn for the end of the half. Out of the corner of his eye, Gipp had caught a momentary glimpse of the official beginning to raise the horn to his lips and knew only a second or two remained. "I've never seen a quicker piece of thinking," commented Rockne afterward, "on the part of a player."

Gameness Wins

Gipp's gameness stood out spectacularly in the game against Indiana in 1920. The Hoosiers showed unexpected power and were leading 13 to 10 with only minutes to go. It looked as though the Irish were beaten. A surge of the old Notre Dame fighting spirit, however, carried the ball to the Indiana seven-yard line. Gipp had been taken from the game with a dislocated shoulder. The substitutes had been exhausted. Gipp came over to Rockne and pleaded to be sent in. There might still be time, he said, to pull the game out of the fire. Reluctantly, the coach yielded.

"He charged on the field," related Rockne, "and the stands rose to acclaim. Rarely have I seen a more thrilling sight than those stands, gaunt in dusk, banked thousands screaming the name of one man—Gipp!

"Of course he was marked. The Indiana men, their first victory over us in thirty years smelling sweet in their nostrils, weren't going to let a crippled hero beat them. But the crippled hero had something to say about that. He tried once—disdaining runs, passing. With a smashed shoulder he smashed the line—and failed. Indiana roared. He tried again. Taking the ball, he crouched into a self-driven battering ram. Smash—and over he went."

It was a display of that game fighting spirit which scorned pain, injury and every obstacle in its path. Bruised and crippled, he reached his brave hand into the fire that October afternoon and pulled victory out of the embracing flames.

Gipp had a marvelous sense of discerning the opponents' attack, and a knack of breaking it up before it got going.

"He was a master of defense," said Rockne, "And I can say of him what cannot, I believe, be said of any other football player, certainly not of any other Notre Dame player—that not a single forward pass was ever completed in territory defended by George Gipp. He had the timing of a tiger in pouncing on its prey. He never missed."

"Tell Them to Go and . . ."

With all his athletic fame, Gipp was the soul of modesty. With the story of his feats spread across the sport pages of the country, with photos of his spectacular open-field running covering half a page, Gipp never read a clipping of a game in which he played. He never posed for a photograph. The only one Rockne had of him was one snapped on the playing field.

At the very zenith of his greatness in 1920, Gipp was stricken with a streptococcus infection which caused his death. The scene at his death bed has become a classic in the annals of gridiron men. It was featured in the cinema, *Rockne—All-American,* and brought moist eyes to broad-shouldered men. It brings out in bold relief the utter gameness of the boy and his smiling courage in the face of death.

"I bent," related Rockne, "over this boy of twenty-three, who had scaled the glamorous heights of all boyhood dreams by shining as a national hero. The White Sox had just bid for his baseball services on graduation. Walter Camp had just named him All-American fullback.

" 'It's pretty tough to go,' said someone at the bedside.

" 'What's tough about it?' Gipp smiled up at us feebly. 'I've no complaint.'

"He turned to me.

"'I've got to go, Rock,' he said. 'It's all right. I'm not afraid.'

"His eyes brightened in a frame of pallor. 'Sometime, Rock,' he said 'when the team's up against it; when things are wrong and the breaks are beating the boys—tell them to go in there with all they've got and win just one for the Gipper. I don't know where I'll be then, Rock. But I'll know about it, and I'll be happy.' "*

"One for the Gipper"

Rockne held the incident in his memory and waited. In 1928 he had to face a punishing schedule with an unusually weak team. It had been cracked by Wisconsin and vanquished by Georgia Tech. It was all but demoralized.

The Army was unusually strong. They had spread devastation among the strongest teams in the East. They were out to give Notre Dame the beating of years. In the first half the Irish had managed with great difficulty to hold the cadets 0-0. But they came in utterly exhausted and all feared they could not much longer stave off the impending defeat.

"For the first time since Gipp's death," related Rockne, "I told the boys what he had said. These lads on that 1928 team had never met Gipp, had never seen him. But Gipp is a legend at Notre Dame. Every football writer at that half time said Notre Dame would be beaten badly. It looked as if we were weakening. But the boys came out for the second half exalted, inspired, overpowering. They

---

* *The Autobiography of Knute K. Rockne,* Indianapolis, Bobbs-Merrill Co., 1930, p. 236.

won. As Chevigny slashed through for the winning touchdown, he said:

" 'That's one for the Gipper!'

"A boy," concluded Rockne, "does well indeed who so young leaves the clean glory of a name behind."

George Gipp has written an epic of sheer gameness and of courage under fire which is as tangible to Notre Dame students as the stones of tradition-dripping Sorin Hall and as lustrous as the golden dome of the Main Building shining in the Hoosier moonlight.

Rockne Speaks

There is another name which spells magic to the students at Notre Dame—the name of Knute Rockne. Acclaimed the master coach of all time, he stands as a symbol of manly vigor, Spartan fortitude, and a courage that found expression in resourcefulness and pluck. Around his name clusters a wealth of memories which are living traditions at Notre Dame and sources of inspiration to the youth of our land.

Let the visitor to Notre Dame step in the Rockne memorial and stand before the bronze likeness of the veteran of many a grueling struggle on the nation's gridirons. A soft amber light from stained glass windows falls upon the face of the grizzled warrior. An atmosphere of cathedral-like reverence envelops him. Against the sounding board of the hallowed traditions of a mighty past, Rockne seems to be uttering anew his warning against the softening influence of modern life and his plea for the toughening of our national fibre through work, hardship and discipline.

"If I have learned any one fact," he is saying again to the educators, "in my twenty years of work with boys, it's this—the most dangerous thing in American life today is that we're getting soft, inside and out! We're losing a forceful heritage of mind and body that was once our most precious possession.

"We—these men [his fellow coaches] and I—have given our lives to working that flaccid philosophy out of our boys' minds and bodies. We believe the finest work of man is building the character of man. We have tried to build courage and initiative, tolerance and persistence, without which the most educated brain in the head of man is not worth very much."

To the rhythm of his thinking and to the pulsing of his fighting heart the students of Notre Dame, coming from every state in the union and from many foreign lands, are endeavoring to walk. His spirit lives on in the coaches directing the athletics of youth in hundreds of colleges and universities today.

Transfer of Training

Thus far, we have presented various instances of courage in the field of sports. One of the prime purposes of athletics is to develop courage, stamina, resourcefulness under fire, but these qualities must not cease when the game is over. They must be woven into the character of the indivdual, they must carry over into the social, civil, and moral life. They must win victories in these vastly more important fields; otherwise, the game would not be worth the candle.

What would be the value of athletics if the individual used his acquired talents only to reap the spoils of corrupt politics, to engage in racketeering and other unwholesome activities with which our cities are infested? What would be the value of competitive sports if the player failed to use his training in the more important contests of fighting the graft, fraud, commercialized vice and crime which are eating like cancer into the very marrow of our urban population? A brain sharpened by training may merely make a more clever criminal, if that training is not illumined by ideals of justice and right.

Participation in competitive sports gives no assurance that the qualities of pluck, stamina and fortitude will be used for the achievement of worthy objectives in the other fields of life, unless that training is lit up with moral ideals. True, most coaches teach their players to fight cleanly, to strive to win honestly, and to prefer defeat to a victory won by cheating. It is of enormous importance that these ideals be made clear, explicit and articulate; otherwise, the transfer of training from the gridiron to the arena of social and political life will be questionable indeed.

That is why school boards and university authorities are generally careful to select a coach who is not only an experienced athlete but a wholesome man. A man of questionable morals has no place in the training of athletes any more than in the work of education. Here, ideals are all-important. If they be lacking or even obscured, the training is likely to be used for unwholesome and unworthy ends.

Athletes who won fame in sports distinguished themselves for bravery in war. Society asks all these men who have proved their mettle against the foe before thousands of spectators to show the same valor, courage and determination in fighting the foes which infest our civilization—the corrupt politicians, gangsters, racketeers and criminals of all descriptions. The F.B.I., among other agencies, is now harnessing in a conspicuous way the valor of young athletes and college graduates in its magnificent battle against criminals.

The Real Battle

America has had for years the unenviable reputation of being the most lawless nation in the world: more murders are perpetrated each year in single cities, such as New York and Chicago, than in all of Great Britain with its population of forty million. If we could fling against the hordes of gangsters and criminals, taking so tremendous an annual toll in life and property from the American people, the army of trained young athletes who fight with the courage of untamed tigers, we would win a victory of major proportions.

What a fine thing it would be if a coach were to say to his players occasionally: "We expect to see you distinguish yourself after you leave this campus by smashing racketeers, tackling gangsters, breaking up the plays of corrupt politicians and parasitic gamblers, and giving no quarter to the moguls of vice and crime. The fury and relentlessness of your attack upon these sinister forces will bring victories more significant than those won on the gridiron. Criminals like John Dillinger, 'Baby Face' Nelson, Al Capone, 'Lucky' Luciano, Roger Banghart, spreading a trail of murder, robbery and corruption in their wake, will challenge the valor and the resourcefulness developed in our sports.

"Show society that you can smash this line with the same fearlessness and determination with which you charge the opposing line in football. The fight for civic decency, for social justice, for political honesty, will pit your courage and your valor against the bulldozing politician, the brass-knuckled racketeers and the machine-gun toting gangsters. That is the struggle which will try your mettle to the limit —a struggle for which these games on the athletic field are but a preparation."

The appeal to all who read these lines, to educators, coaches, students, and men and women in every walk of life, is to focus so enormous an emphasis upon the ideals of private honesty and civic decency, of fairness and honor in all the relationships of life, that the education of youth will inevitably reflect that emphasis. Educators and coaches will be helped immensely in their task of guiding the young in carrying over the ideals of the classroom and of the athletic field into the great arena of life, if they are backed by the power of an aroused public opinion.

Courage on the athletic field should be viewed as preparation for valor in the social and civil arenas. Unless it is carried over to fight the real enemies of society, athletics become merely a game of blindman's buff. Ideals must so impregnate the education of youth that the muscles of the will and the sinews of character are developed no less effectively than the muscles of the body.

Summary

To sum up. Since courage is a habit, it is subject to the laws of habit formation. Basic among those laws is the one which stresses the importance and the necessity of repeating an act to render it habitual. Competitive sports provide abundant opportunity for individuals to face opposition and, after analyzing it, to react with courage and resourcefulness. Such habits should be carried over to the tasks of business, professional, civic and political life. The field of sports thus becomes the training ground for the conscientious and courageous fulfillment of the important duties of life.

RULE 3. *Make all games and contests serve as occasions for the formation of the habit of courage in the face of difficulty and competition in the serious tasks of life, whether they be landing a job, earning a living, proposing to your sweetheart.*

Reflect upon the instances of courage cited in this chapter and wait until tomorrow to read the next chapter.

CHAPTER FOUR

CONQUERING NEW WORLDS

Earth shakes beneath them, and heaven roars above;
But nothing scares them from the course they love.
—Cowper, *Table Talk.*

COURAGE IS DEVELOPED *through the performance of deeds in spite of difficulty and opposition. The accomplishment of such feats in the field of competitive sports or in other domains leads to the habit of courageous action. There are other fields of activity, studded with deeds of gallantry and endurance, which few of us are likely to traverse. They are the fields of discovery and exploration.*

The reading of the feats of such intrepid pioneers blazing new trails on earth and in the sky can nevertheless assist in the development of courage. How? By enabling us to see how men can withstand hardship, brave peril, endure privation and suffer agony for the achievement of a goal. The subordination of personal comfort for the attainment of a larger end constitutes the core of courage. Such subordination is vividly and often dramatically depicted in the efforts of stout-hearted pioneers to open new worlds to mankind.

No reader can accompany these intrepid adventurers on their perilous journeys and witness the stamina with which they endured hardship and suffering, the pluck with which they pushed on to their goal, without finding himself saying: "If these men could endure such trials with patience and surmount such obstacles without faltering, I can carry my much lighter burdens with manliness and courage. By patience, resourcefulness and determination, I, too, can achieve my goal."

Hence, a brief presentation of some of the highlights of the achievements of the fearless charters of new trails across the trackless wilderness of the world will help both to inspire the attitude and to inculcate the practice of courage.

Hardship and Danger

The field of exploration and discovery is a domain where courage and fortitude have found frequent expression. The very nature of the work attracts the more venturesome and courageous spirits. The enterprise is studded with hardships and dangers which challenge the resourcefulness and the intrepidity of the explorers. The blazing of new trails through uncharted regions of polar ice, through primaeval jungles, through unexplored skies is no pastime for timid souls. The peril of death that stares in the face the voyager through new worlds at nearly every turn is enough to freeze the blood and stop the beating of the heart of the timorous.

The domain of the unexplored, with all its lurking dangers and unforeseen obstacles, is the natural testing ground of the qualities of the stout heart and the intrepid soul. Like the proving ground, with its obstacle course of hill, ditch, mud and water, on which are tested the pulling powers of a new motor, the unmapped regions of earth and sea constitute nature's own testing ground of fortitude and courage. Stamina, gameness, endurance, resourcefulness and, above all, stout-hearted courage are called for in abundance.

The lure of the unexplored, like the lure of the forbidden fruit, has from time immemorial exercised its spell upon mankind, enticing them to blaze new trails through strange lands and untraversed seas. Into those uncharted regions adventurers disappear to return no more. Does that daunt others? On the contrary, it seems to add new and irresistible lure to the conquest of territory which made but graves for the hardy explorers who sought to pierce the veil wrapped around it by the centuries.

Thus, when John Cabot sailed with his fleet of five vessels from Bristol in 1498 to explore the far north of the American continent, only to be swallowed up in its white immensities, other adventurers in different lands sprang up to meet the challenge of the ice-locked northern seas. The greater the difficulties and the more harrowing the experiences of the early explorers, the more luring became the challenge to pit human bravery and resourcefulness against the raging blizzards, the menacing icebergs, and the piercing cold of the arctic.

Those Who Pay the Toll

The willingness of venturesome spirits to gamble life and limb in the effort to fill in some of the blank spaces in our maps of land, sea, and air has been the necessary antecedent to man's conquest of the strange globe upon which he dwells. The shoving back of the frontiers of our darkness was not accomplished without its toll of suffering and death. The gallant band who paid the toll, while not unmindful of the gratitude of posterity, seem to have found in the struggle which stretched the tether of their courage and endurance to the breaking point, a large, if not a complete, measure of their recompense.

"Bring on your blinding blizzards, your ice-locked seas, your polar bears, your desolate wastes, your treacherous crevasses, your numbing cold, your eternal snow and ice, your long black night. I'll conquer them all!" Such seems to have been the challenge which the Arctic adventurer hurled at the far north.

It is a spectacle which provokes the admiration of mankind and makes even the more timorous among us rejoice that the iron chord of courage is vibrating so vigorously in human souls. Even when we cannot respond with equally strong notes, we are not unconscious of an antiphonal note echoing in our own souls—a note which may grow stronger, and mature full-orbed, after immersing ourselves in the stern melodies of courage, gallantry and daring played by the explorers of unmapped worlds.

Piled high on my desk, as I write, is a heap of volumes recording the struggles and feats of explorers in many fields. Some speak of those who came to grips with the cruelty and the grandeur of the Arctic, of others who turned later on to the challenge of the ruthlessness and the majesty of the Antarctic, and of those who braved the lurking perils of the African jungle. Other volumes tell of the adventurers into the new region of the air, seeking by this new means to span the oceans and to fly above the poles. Still others chronicle man's effort to explore the mysterious life which thrives in the ocean's depths—the last domain to yield its secrets to man's adventurous spirit.

The stories of all these adventurers sound the general notes of courage and endurance. Each group, however, seems to sound its own distinctive overtone in the varied orchestration of gameness, fortitude, the patient endurance of frightful hardships, resourcefulness under fire, and a boldness that flung defiance at all the winds that blow.

The Challenge of the Arctic

First, let us glance at some of the struggles to penetrate into the frozen north, for that was the scene of some of the earliest explorations. Looking back more than a thousand years into the chronicles of the past, we find one of the earliest records at the time when King Alfred sat upon the English throne. Residing at the court of Alfred, about the year 890, was a hardy Norwegian named Othar, who felt, as he relates, "a desire to learn how far the land stretched towards the north, and if there were any regions inhabited by man northward beyond the desert waste."

He sailed into the unexplored regions of the north and on his return reported the results of his discoveries to the king. Thus, Othar the Norwegian made the first recorded entrance into the Arctic sea, while King Alfred of England, who placed on record the results of the voyage, appears to have been the earliest chronicler of Arctic adventure.

About a century elapsed before the curtain was again

raised upon ventures into the polar sea. A bold Icelandic rover, Eric the Red, prepared a vessel and, sailing with his followers in a westerly course, came in sight of the east coast of Greenland, along which he steered southwards, looking for a habitable spot. After exploring the western coast of Greenland, he returned to Iceland. He made so favorable a report of the new country that he induced a large body of colonists to sail with him in 985 in twenty-five ships. About half of the fleet perished in the ice-locked sea, but the remnant reached their destination. Within a few years settlers were to be found in all the habitable places of Greenland.

Columbus Blazes a Trail

There follows a curious lapse of five centuries, during which little seems to have been done to wrest from the Arctic the secrets she had hidden so long. The epochal voyage of Christopher Columbus gave birth to a spirit of exploration and discovery which was to send hardy adventurers roaming through the vast wilderness of the New World. The achievement of Columbus was the culmination of many years of persistent effort and the materialization of a dream that would not die.

The picture of this brave captain, standing at the prow of the *Santa Maria,* scanning the shoreless seas, and directing his vessel onward into waters where no ship had ever sailed, is a picture of courage lighted by the flame of a great conviction. Not even the threat of mutiny could swerve him from his onward course. He gave to humanity a New World. He taught us likewise one of the noblest lessons that man can teach — the invincible might of a courage that never falters. The most memorable voyage of discovery in the history of the world was accomplished at an expense of about $22,115. Contrast with this the sum of more than half a million dollars which Commander Byrd spent on his trip to the South Pole.

Following in the wake of Columbus were many voyages to the New World. The literature of that day shows that the goal of many was a Northwest Passage to India and China. The southern routes, east by the Cape of Good Hope, and west by Cape Horn, were long and dangerous. If a way could be found in the north, it would be a great boon to merchants and traders. For several centuries sturdy mariners embarked on the perilous undertaking of finding that passage. It led them into the Arctic regions, where their struggles with the elements were to write new classics in the long story of man's battle with the forces of the unconquered North.

Hudson's Tragic Fate

Let us glance briefly at a few episodes in the struggle to wrest the secrets of the Arctic from her icy grip. They will disclose the type of obstacles and the hardships which had to be surmounted by those who ventured into her trackless wastes. Sailing from England in 1607, on the first of his expeditions into the polar seas, Henry Hudson discovered the abundance of whales in the northern waters, and his report led to the beginning of the great whale industry. On a subsequent voyage while in search of the Northwest Passage he discovered, emptying into New

York bay, the noble river to which his name was given.

His fourth voyage forms a tragic chapter in the history of Arctic exploration. He penetrated along the coast of Labrador and, still in search of the Northwest Passage, entered into the great inland sea which came to be known as Hudson Bay. The rigors of a northern winter held him and his crew in the ice, while their scanty provisions became increasingly inadequate. He continued to explore the country, straining his eyes for an outlet to the western sea, but in vain.

His crew became mutinous and, despite his own cheerful and courageous attitude, proceeded to carry out one of the blackest pieces of treachery in the annals of the Arctic. They placed Hudson, his son, and the sick in a boat with only two days' provisions and set them adrift. In what form death came to relieve their sufferings no one knows. The name of Hudson looms large, however, in the history of Arctic exploration and stands to this day as a symbol of courage.

"I Shall Go Back"

Another record of courage was written in the annals of the Arctic by the feat of an English midshipman, Hearne, who had come to America and entered the Hudson Bay Company's service. At the age of 24, in 1771, he was sent out with four companions to find the Northwest Passage.

Dragging a single sledge loaded with provisions, they started out on their long trek across the treeless waste now called Mackenzie, which skirts the Arctic circle. They were without dogs and without a tent. They camped in the desolate waste, swept by raging blizzards. Bitterly were they to rue their decision not to bring a tent, when the pair who were assigned to keep guard were found frozen stiff in the morning.

When his companions, unwilling any longer to endure the rigors of the arctic, deserted him, Hearne treked on alone. Without arms or provisions in a trackless waste, exposed to danger from polar bears and hostile Indians, with only his compass to guide him, Hearne pushed on. "Tasting nothing the while," he tells us, "but a few cranberries, water, melted snow or ice, scraps of leather and burnt bones," he struggled on until he reached Fort Prince of Wales a living skeleton, scarcely able to stand. "I shall go back next year," he said, "if I die by the way."

Next spring he ventured forth from the gates of the fort alone. With the aid of friendly Indians whom he encountered, he explored vast stretches of territory, coming at last to what he thought was the "Hyperborean Sea" —the farthest limit of the north of America. All his troubles, hardships, and his 1300-mile trek seemed as nothing, he said, in the light of that discovery. He had spent four years in the Arctic wastes, a considerable portion of that period alone, and brought back to civilization an amazing story of what the human body can endure when it is armored with courage. His experience would seem to demonstrate the truth of Dryden's words:

Presence of mind and courage in distress,
Are more than armies to procure success.

The Explorer's Pest

We are accustomed to think of the raging blizzards and the piercing cold as sources of the greatest discomfort to explorers in the far north. But in the summer there is a source of even greater vexation — the mosquito, the pest of the explorer in all climes. Hood draws a vivid picture of the agony inflicted by swarms of these little beasts: "We had sometimes before procured a little rest by closing the tent and burning wood or flashing gunpowder within, the smoke driving the mosquitoes into the crannies of the ground. But this remedy was not effectual, though we employed it so perseveringly as to hazard suffocation; they swarmed under our blankets, goring us with their envenomed trunks and steeping our clothes in blood. We rose at daylight in a fever, and our misery was unmitigated during our whole stay."

The mosquito can bore through the hide of a buffalo. If not disturbed, it will gorge itself with blood until its body swells into a transparent globe. The wound caused by the Arctic mosquito does not swell, like that caused by the African variety, but its wound is vastly more painful. When multiplied many times, and continued for successive days, these sores become a greater torture than the worst blizzards which sweep across the Arctic.

Swarms of mosquitoes drive the buffaloes to the plains, irritating them to madness. They chase the reindeer into the sea, from which they do not emerge until the scourge has ceased. The waning of the winter, instead of bringing some relief for the explorer, unleashes upon him a more vexatious enemy and one that is ruthless in its gluttonous persistence.

Risking Lives for Others

In 1883, Greeley was exploring around Eskimo Point. At midnight he was awakened by the sound of the staggering footsteps of a messenger. Elison, one of Greeley's group at Rosse Bay, was dying. Without loss of time, his little band, though half-starved themselves and enfeebled by a long march, hastened with food and medicine in a desperate dash to succor their dying comrade. Traveling in darkness over rough and broken ice, they made a journey of forty miles in forty-four hours.

They found Elison and his two companions in a desperate plight. The sleeping bag had frozen solid, holding the three helpless men rigid in the one position for eighteen hours. The bag had to be cut to release them. The medical supplies, the food and the ministrations of the rescuers enabled Elison to edge slowly out of his critical illness. In his journal Greeley says of the rescuing party: "They had been on reduced rations for over two months, and although unfit for the most ordinary service, they ventured their lives cheerfully on the barest possibility of rescuing a comrade."

Later on, two of his men, Rice and Frederick, volunteered to do some particularly dangerous exploring. Because of a raging blizzard, they could not locate a cache of provisions, and were reduced to a pitiable condition. Rice was unable to stand. Lying on the sledge, he awaited the end. In spite of the raging storm, Frederick removed some of his own clothing and wrapped the garments around the dying man. Seated on the sledge in his shirt-sleeves, he held his comrade in his arms until his eyes closed in death.

Then he struggled, half-frozen, half-famished and completely exhausted, back to the base camp. Knowing that they, too, were on exceedingly reduced rations, Frederick, though half-starved, brought back the rations which had been allocated to his dead companion that he might share them with the others. Here are loyalty, nobility of character, and gallantry of a high degree. The annals of the north are full of such instances.

Peary Achieves Goal

The first man to reach the north pole, according to many historians, was Robert E. Peary. For twenty-three years he had been struggling with courage and resourcefulness to reach this coveted goal. Obstacles and difficulties confronted him to the very end. When near the end of their long march, they encountered a strip of thin ice about a hundred yards wide.

"As I ran ahead to guide the dogs," says Peary, "I was obliged to slide my feet and travel wide, bear style, in order to distribute my weight. The last two men came over on all fours. I watched them from the other side with my heart in my mouth — watched the ice bending under the weight of the sledges and men. As one of the sledges neared the northside, a runner cut clear through the ice, and I expected every moment that the whole thing, dogs and all, would go through the ice and down to the bottom. But it did not."

A disaster such as that would have frustrated all their hopes and doubtless have taken their lives as well. But courage, buttressed with determination and perseverence, finally won. The pole grudgingly yielded the secrets she had held so long in her icy bosom.

On April 6, 1909, Peary, Hensen and his Eskimos stood where no human foot had ever trodden before. It was the culmination of four hundred years of exploration.

"East, West and North," relates Peary, "had disappeared for us. Only one direction remained and that was South. Where we were, one day and one night constituted a year, a hundred such days and nights constituted a century."

It was a superb achievement. Baffled again and again, Peary refused to accept defeat. The untamed Arctic had permitted adventurers to penetrate into her icy lair, but in due time she had caught up with all of them and halted them before they reached their goal. Undismayed by all these defeats, Peary persisted with an iron-willed determination that nothing could daunt. The story of his conquest is a saga of courage lit up by intelligence and buttressed by an indomitable will.

The perfection of the airplane after World War I placed in the hands of Arctic explorers an instrument of amazing power and revolutionized the methods of reaching the pole. In 1926, Commander Byrd, with Bennett, as his pilot flew over the pole. Shortly afterwards, Amudsen and Ellsworth accomplished the same feat in a dirigible.

The Antarctic Beckons

Attempts to penetrate the Antarctic began much later

and were much fewer. In 1909, Ernest Shackleton penetrated to within 100 miles of the South Pole. At this point, they encountered a raging blizzard, suffered attacks of dysentery, and were further weakened from lack of sufficient food. To proceed further under such circumstances would mean that they would not come back alive. It was a heart-breaking disappointment. But Shackleton wisely decided to start the return trek.

Before reaching their ship, Marshall became so ill that he could proceed no farther. Leaving the sick man in the care of Adams, Shackleton and Wild made a forced march of thirty-three miles to the ship. Shackleton had been without sleep for twenty-four hours. He might well have assigned the task of rescuing the two men left behind to other members of the crew.

Taking time only to eat a hasty meal, however, Shackleton set out with medicine and supplies to rescue his two comrades who were hourly growing weaker. After traveling for a day and a half, he reached them and succeeded in bringing them safely back to the ship. With little sleep, he had covered ninety-nine miles in three days, at the end of an exhausting march of 1700 miles. Here is an achievement that ranks among the great feats of courage and pluck with which polar enterprise abounds.

A Tragic Chapter

The most moving and tragic chapter in the annals of antarctic exploration, however, was that written by Capt. Richard F. Scott and his comrades. An English seaman of marked intelligence and courage, Scott had penetrated in

1903 deep into the Antarctic continent. Seven years later he determined to return and try to reach the pole, which had thus far defeated all such attempts. Setting out in June, 1910, Scott pushed his way deep into the Antarctic. By January 3, 1912, he reached a latitude of 87° 32 S and with four picked men made a resolute march for the Pole.

Threading their way around treacherous crevasses and pressure ridges, they maintained an average of twelve miles a day until they reached the pole on January 17, 1912. To their intense chagrin, they found that Amundsen had beaten them by a month. For there in the desolate waste was the tell-tale evidence — Amundsen's tent and records claiming the territory for Norway and naming the plateau in honor of its sovereign, King Haakon VII. After all their struggle, their conquest of the pole, they felt, was now a barren honor.

"It is a terrible disappointment," wrote Scott in his journal, "and I am very sorry for my loyal companions."

For two days they remained at the pole, resting, making observations, leaving records, and planting the British flag near that of Norway. Then they started the long trek back.

At first, the weather conditions were favorable, and good progress was made over the polar plateau. But soon, sterner conditions confronted them. The surfaces became more difficult, and the descent of the Beardmore Glacier was rendered hazardous by the falling snow which enabled them to glimpse only occasionally the surrounding land.

A still greater peril confronted them, however, in the signs of weakness which Evans, the strong man of the party, began to show. In the descent of the glacier, Evans fell among the heavy ice, sustaining a bad head injury. With a weak and injured comrade on their hands, the others were compelled to slow their pace. This meant that their food was to suffer an unexpected diminution. Finally, Evans became so weak that he was unable to stumble further along. His comrades carried him on the sledge until he died, February 17, at the foot of Beardmore Glacier.

"I May Be Some Time"

The terrible strain was beginning to tell on the survivors, especially on Captain Oates, who had been struggling on despite badly frost-bitten hands and feet. By March 16 it was obvious that the end of the trail for him was rapidly approaching.

"He was a brave soul," wrote Captain Scott in recording his death. "He slept through the night hoping not to wake, but he awoke in the morning. It was blowing a blizzard, Oates said, 'I am going outside, and I may be some time.' He went out into the blizzard, and we have not seen him since. We knew that Oates was walking to his death, but though we tried to dissuade him, we knew it was the act of a brave man and an English gentleman."

While a question might possibly be raised concerning the ethical complexion of Oates' action considered objectively, the captain appears to have considered it in the line of heroic duty. In walking out alone into the howling blizzard, thus increasing the food allotments for the remaining three, and relieving them of a burden which promised to prove fatal to all, Oates hoped he would afford the others a fighting chance, while his was somewhat less.*

Scott and his two companions once more pushed on as fast as the bad weather conditions permitted. After five days of struggling onward through the snow and ice, their strength was gone and they were forced to camp. Only eleven miles away was the One Ton Camp, where food and fuel awaited them. Meanwhile, the blizzard continued to rage around their little tent with undiminished fury. They had reached the end of the trail. One by one, they ebbed away into the sleep that knows no waking.

Months later, a searching party found their bodies. Wilson and Bowers were lying in the sleeping bags which proved to be their shrouds. Scott, apparently the last to die, was sitting with his back to the tent pole, with his diary resting between him and the pole. The pencil had fallen from frozen fingers as he wrote farewell to the world.

Scott's Last Farewell

The final struggle is thus disclosed in the diary:

"I do not think human beings ever came through such a month as we have come through; and we should have got through, in spite of the weather, but for the sickening of a second companion, Captain Oates, and a shortage of fuel in our depots for which I cannot account; and finally, but for the storm which has fallen on us within eleven

* Henry Davis, S.J., in his *Moral and Pastoral Theology* (Vol. II, p. 145), justifies Oates on the ground of primary intention, his death not being the motive on which he acted.

miles of the depot at which we hoped to secure the final supplies.

"Surely misfortune could scarcely have exceeded this last blow. We arrived within eleven miles of our old One Ton Camp with fuel for one hot meal and food for two days.

"For four days we have been unable to leave the tent, a gale blowing about us.

"We are weak, writing is difficult, but for my own sake I do not regret this journey, which has shown us that Englishmen can endure hardships, help one another, and meet death with as great fortitude as ever in the past.

"We took risks — we know we took them.

"Things have come out against us, and therefore we have no cause for complaint, but bow to the will of Providence, determined still to do our best to the last . . .

"Had we lived I should have had a tale to tell of the hardihood, endurance, and courage of my companions which would have stirred the heart of every Englishman."

The Authentic Mark

Along with his diary was found a farewell note to his friend, Sir James M. Barrie. "We are pegging out," he wrote, "in a very comfortless spot. Hoping this letter may be found and sent to you, I write you a word of farewell. I want you to think well of me and my end.

"Good-bye — I am not at all afraid of the end, but sad to miss many a simple pleasure which I had planned for the future in our long marches . . . . We are in a desperate state — feet frozen, etc., no fuel, and a long way from food, but it would do your heart good to be in our tent, to hear our songs and cheery conversation."

Here is the authentic mark of courage — facing insurmountable odds with cheerfulness, and smiling in the face of death. One of the highest forms of courage is that which takes defeat with a smile and thereby transforms it into victory.

Stand by that tent on the bleak Antarctic. Outside you hear the howling fury of the blizzard hurling its vengeance upon those who have penetrated to its deepest lair. Inside you hear no complaining, no cries of petulance, but "songs and cheery conversation." The elements of the Antarctic can crush the bodies of men, but they stand in mute impotence before the naked might of the human soul.

Scott's end calls to mind the story of the youth who fell down an Alpine glacier and was lost. One of his youthful companions of a scientific turn of mind computed that the body would appear at a certain date and place many years later. When that time arrived, some of the survivors, now old men, returned to the glacier to see if the prediction would be fulfilled. To their surprise, the body reappeared as young as on the day he left them. So Scott and his companions step once again out of the white immensities — always young.

Barrie related the incident of Scott and his companions in a rectorial address to the students of St. Andrews University, and added: "How comely a thing is affliction borne cheerfully, which is not beyond the reach of the humblest of us. What is beauty? It is these hard-bitten men singing courage to you from their tent; it is the waves of their island home crooning of their deeds to you who are to follow them. Sometimes beauty boils over and then spirits are abroad. Ages may pass as we look or listen, for time is annihilated."*

Indeed, the smile of courage in the face of death may be said to be the expression of the soul's intuition of its own immortality — the confident intimation that even if the bark sinks, it sinks to another shore.

A perusal of the diaries of these hardy adventurers into the polar seas discloses that they turned to God in prayer in time of emergency. "In my distress," writes Amundsen, "I sent up (I honestly confess it) an ardent prayer to the Almighty." In that simple line is mirrored the experience of practically every explorer who finds himself in a desperate plight. When man has his back to the wall, he finds himself turning to God for strength to endure, to struggle, to fight through to victory. Courage is a spiritual quality which has its mountainhead in God. Prayer is the channel through which it streams to us.

"Greatest Individual Feat"

Let us turn now to explorers in other fields. Foremost among those who have blazed new trails in the skies is Charles A. Lindbergh. "The greatest individual feat in all history," said Commander Byrd of the Lone Eagle's flight from New York to Paris. He covered a distance of 3,600 miles in 33½ hours. For more than a thousand miles he had to battle fog, rain and sleet. He displayed not only

* *Courage,* New York, Charles Scribner's Sons, 1923.

great mechanical ability but a courage illuminated with intelligence and fortified by careful planning.

"They call me lucky," remarked Lindbergh, "but luck is not enough. As a matter of fact, I had what I regarded as the best existing plane for the purpose of my flight, and I was equipped with what were, in the circumstances, the best possible instruments for making the flight. I hope I made good use of what I had."

Lindbergh was but twenty-five when he made that epochal flight on May 20, 1927. While his take-off was preceded by careful planning and the rigorous inspection of his machine, for which he is noted, there was unquestionably a dash of youthful daring in the undertaking. That Lindbergh was hazarding his life to chart a new path through the skies, a path that would bind the New World more closely with the Old, was clear even to himself.

"I am entering my death chamber," he remarked as he climbed into the cockpit. "If I arrive in Paris, it will be like receiving a pardon from the Governor." Yet, with the daring characteristic of youth, he did not hesitate to take the long end of the odds and prove that he could win.

A wave of exultation swept across the nation and over the whole of Europe when the news of his safe arrival at LeBourget Field was flashed to an astonished world. The welcome which was accorded him upon his return to New York has probably never been equaled. Offers from Hollywood, from theatres and other agencies seeking to exploit his gallant feat, poured in upon him like a tidal wave. Fortunes were dangled before him as inducements. With characteristic modesty, however, Lindbergh turned a deaf ear to all of them. He was no fortune hunter. His was the answer of youth to the age-old challenge of the Atlantic and to the uncharted skies above it.

This spectacular achievement, along with his other notable pioneering in the skies of other regions, will long remain an inspiration to the courage of the youth of America and of the world. My own personal contact with the noted flier has served to give me an added appreciation of his modesty—which sits like a crown upon the brow of heroes — and to enhance still further my high admiration of his courage and ability.

Livingstone in Africa

Africa had been for centuries a vast *terra incognita.* Only its fringes had been explored; its interior was a land of darkness and of mystery. The man whose name is forever associated with the exploration of the African jungle is Dr. David Livingstone. A native of Scotland, Livingstone sailed for South Africa in 1840, arriving at the little port of Cape Town at the southern tip of the continent after a three months voyage. For thirty-three years he struggled through the swamps and the jungles, the mountains and the rivers of central Africa. He penetrated into regions and visited tribes where no white man had ever been.

He was exposed to the perils of man-eating lions, deadly snakes, poisonous insects, and murderous tribes. How he survived all these dangers, each of which has proven fatal to so many travelers, is indeed difficult to understand. Not only did he overcome these, but he brought to many of the natives some of the ways of life of the white man's civilization. He became among them an apostle of healing and of light. He afforded the world for the first time a comprehensive and accurate picture of the Congo. He discovered the second largest river in the world, the Congo, which he thought to be the Nile.

For some years no word was heard of Livingstone. Whether he was alive or dead, the outside world could not tell. In 1871, the New York *Herald* organized an expedition, headed by Henry Stanley, to search for the missing explorer. The meeting of the two men on the shores of Lake Tanganyika is one of the dramatic incidents in the annals of African exporation. Declining the invitation to return, Livingstone stayed at his self-appointed post of duty till his death in 1873.

His explorations covered one-third of the continent, extending from the Cape to near the equator, and from the Atlantic to the Indian Ocean. His sympathy and kindness won the natives, and he so aroused the indignation of England against the traffic in slaves as to lead to determined and, to a considerable extent, successful efforts to get the Sultan of Zanzibar to suppress the trade. His journal tells a tale of suffering and of hardships which will equal, if not surpass, that of the polar explorer.

Early in his career he was attacked by a lion which crushed his left arm. As the bone was improperly set, the arm was a source of trouble to him at times throughout his life. He suffered the frequent plague of mosquitoes and of insects, endured the fever of the swamps, and illnesses for which he had no name, until his once iron frame was reduced to "a ruckle of bones." "That's courage," observed the Roman dramatist, Titus Plautus, before the Christian era, "to take hard knocks like a man when occasion calls." Livingstone quietly took all the beating that an African jungle can give. Courage walked with him all the way.

He wrote a chapter in the history of African exploration which is shot through with the bright colors of unselfishness, devotion to duty, and the brave facing of almost daily peril. "In the annals of exploration of the Dark Continent," wrote Stanley, "we look in vain among other nationalities for a name such as Livingstone's. He stands pre-eminent above all; he unites in himself all the best qualities of other explorers." The motto of his life was: "Fear God and work hard."

Courage Conquers All Things

What part of the globe remains to challenge the adventurous spirit of man? While most of the map has been filled in, there still remain areas in Africa, Asia, and the polar seas to be laid bare. The stratosphere still challenges man to new heights to discover more about the mysterious cosmic rays which stream from interstellar space through our atmosphere. The vast depths of the ocean lure us to investigate the finny life that is teeming there.

Already, Beebe's explorations along the floor of the Gulf of Gonaive in Haiti are introducing us to some of the marvels of the land of Jules Verne. I saw some of the pictures which Beebe took in his diving box, showing a huge jelly-fish carrying along little living fishes within its own transparent self, and fiddler crabs carrying on courtships ridiculously like our own. It is a foretaste of new enchantments from the hidden life of the seas, when the diving and photographic techniques become perfected.

"We stand on the threshold of a new era of scientific exploration which is just as romantic, just as alluring, and just as adventurous as that of Peary and Amundsen, of Stanley and Hedin," observes the explorer, Roy Chapman Andrews, in his volume, *On the Trail of Ancient Man.* Never will dawn the day when the insatiable curiosity of man will not find a new frontier for adventurous spirits to explore. Fortified with ever increasing efficient technical equipment and with the might of invincible courage, man will march on to the conquest of new worlds. Now, as in the days of Caesar, courage conquers all things.

Summary

Fortitude, stamina and pluck are important ingredients of courage. These qualities are portrayed in vivid and sometimes dramatic fashion by explorers, adventurers and discoverers. Their feats drive home to all of us the sobering truth that new continents and new seas were brought within the ken of humanity only through the sacrifices, hardships and indomitable courage of sturdy souls. The blazing of new trails is shown to be replete with danger and to call for grit, endurance and determination. We all can gain insight and inspiration from the achievements of pathfinders and trail blazers in the less spectacular but not less important tasks which fill our days. Courage and resourcefulness will pay not less dividends to us than to the adventurers into new worlds.

The feats of explorers and discoverers disclose vividly the core of courage — the subordination of personal comfort for the attainment of a larger end. The reading of the lives of the saints is helpful in inspiring Christians with the will to imitate their holy deeds. Similarly, the perusal of the achievements of explorers and discoverers inspires readers to face their tasks with courage and to press on with fortitude and determination to their accomplishment.

Such absorption with the feats of sturdy pioneers floods the mind of the reader with a psychic atmosphere of dauntless intrepidity and invincible courage which generates similar attitudes, practices and habits. After reading about such deeds, he finds himself saying: "If they could bear such hardships and overcome such obstacles to reach their goal, I can do likewise. Away with the jitters, the fears and the dreads which scare me stiff and paralyze the nerves of action! On with the armor of courage, and I shall fight through to victory!"

RULE 4. *Draw inspiration and courage from the deeds of stout-hearted explorers and adventurers who allowed no obstacle or hardship to swerve them from the achievement of their goal; read of their stirring feats of endurance and valor when fear is seeking to cross the threshold of your mind and you will find it beating a quick and shameful retreat.*

Reflect upon the instances of courage cited in this chapter and wait until tomorrow to read the next chapter.

CHAPTER FIVE

THE COURAGE OF SCHOLARS

Fortitudo, eam virtutem propugnantem pro aequitate.
Courage is that virtue which champions the cause of right.
— Cicero, *De Officiis*

WHILE FEW WILL HAVE THE OPPORTUNITY *of exploring uncharted areas of the globe or of filling in blank spaces in the world's map, all have occasion to do some hard thinking to solve problems which confront them ever and anon. Is there a role for courage to play in enterprises of an intellectual character? Indeed there is—and an important one. In the accomplishment of intellectual feats, courage is not less essential than in those of a physical character. It is required not only by the artist, the scholar, the scientist, but also by the ordinary person who must solve the problems which each day brings to him. Hence, the development of intellectual courage is of prime importance for all.*

How can it be developed? By substantially the same methods by which the other forms of courage are developed. Basic in the development of every kind of courage is the frank facing of difficulty. Instead of running away from it and forgetting it, as popular psychology counsels, one must turn and confront the difficulty. He must analyze the problem into its elementts and face each one of them with calmness, understanding and patience; insight comes as the end product of sustained attention.

From such dispassionate and careful study of a situation an individual gradually comes to perceive the best method of attacking it. But the fire must be withheld until the target is clearly seen. "Be sure you're right," Abraham Lincoln was wont to say, "then go ahead." The most serious and sustained thought of which an individual is capable must be focused upon a problem before he mobilizes his forces for assault. Every form of courage has eyes, but in the domain of intellectual endeavor the eyes must be used until light floods every crevice of the problem.

In addition to using the technique of turning and confronting the problem, the scholar must secure a clear perception of the ideal which will supply motive power and driving force to stick unremittingly at the task until the solution has been reached. It is through the clear envisagement of the ideal that the scholar, the artist, the scientist derives the will to win. With the artist the ideal is beauty; with the scientist, it is truth. These are the ideals which the scholar pursues with the pluck, stamina, fortitude and determination with which the explorer and discoverer push on to untrodden areas on land and sea and in the skies.

The imprisonment of beauty in verse and in prose, on canvas and in stone, is the object of the artist's endless quest. The distillation of truth from the phenomena of nature and the reduction of the multiplicity of nature's myriad activities to the unity of law are the objects for which the scientist strives with tireless patience. In proportion to the accuracy with which each person solves his work-a-day problems does he too come into possession of truth and beauty as well as peace of mind. In the methods pursued by Mendel, Fabre, Pasteur, Newton, Parkman and Michelangelo the reader will find not only the technique but also the spirit and the ideals which enabled them to achieve their long-sought goals. In the stories of their strivings, the reader will find the secret of courage.

Intellectual Courage

Back of most of the great discoveries which have blazed new paths through the jungles of ignorance and the wilderness of superstition has been the courage of a mind struggling for truth and light. No less important for the welfare of the race than physical courage is intellectual courage. It is akin to moral courage, which fights for its convictions against social pressure. We use the term intellectual courage to indicate that inner quality which prompts men to struggle with might and main and endless labor for the discovery of truth in all the fields of science and the achievement of beauty in all the domains of art and letters.

The exercise of physical courage is usually visible. The functioning of intellectual courage is rarely perceptible. In the early stages of World War I, Foch is said to have sent the following message to General Joffre: "My right wing is dangerously threatened. My center is giving away. It is impossible for me to move. The situation is excellent. I shall attack with all force." The gallant courage of Foch and the valorous deeds of his soldiers are written on the pages of an open book for all the world to read and admire.

The courage of the searcher for the truths locked in the arcana of nature is usually hidden, however, in the obscurity of the laboratory or in the fields of natural research. That of the artist finds expression in the striving for form and color in the undramatic studio. The literateur fights his brave battle bent over a lonely, unglamorous desk. The paths of these searchers for truth and beauty are strewn with the boulders of unremitting toil and the thorns and briars of infinite care and a patience that never ends.

True, now and then a name bursts into fame through a spectacular discovery, but for the most part, the workers toil away in their laboratories, grateful if their lives' labors will clear the way for some future researcher to reach the long sought goal. Like Moses, they journey in the desert and never enter into the Promised Land, thankful for a distant view of it from Mount Nebo. The discoveries are nearly always the flowers which bloom upon the long stem of the labors of myriad workers in the field. That is part of the nobility and unselfishness of scientists.

Gregor Mendel

They are happy in searching for the truth, striving to tease out a law from the tangled phenomena of nature. If they do not succeed themselves, they are happy in the knowledge that their labors may constitute the foundation for a fellow worker's success. It is truth that matters. The glory of the individuals in the army of workers who contribute to its ultimate discovery fortunately does not much concern them. That is their least concern. Here is intellectual courage that wears the lowly garb of humility, one of the loveliest of all the virtues.

Abbot Gregor Mendel worked away with his experiments on rough and smooth peas in the garden of his monastery at Bruenn, Austria, for eight years, till he teased out of their variations important laws of genetics. His work laid the scientific foundation for the analytical and biomathematical treatment of the problem of heredity. He published his discoveries in 1865 in the journal of the local natural history society. He carried on a long correspondence with the distinguished botanist, C. Von Naegeli, but he could not interest the latter in his findings.

It was not until 1900, sixteen years after the abbot's death, that the scientific world finally perceived the far-reaching character of his discoveries and paid tardy homage to his genius. Abbot Mendel was working not for the world's acclaim; like all consecrated souls, he was working for the discovery of truth. Though his contemporaries failed to recognize the epochal nature of his discoveries, he had the satisfaction in the inner citadel of his soul of looking into the radiant face of truth and of unveiling that face for all the world finally to gaze upon. More than that no man can do.

Jean Henri Fabre

Jean Henri Fabre came to know more about the ways of insects than any man in France. His key to the door that opened upon that mysterious world was an unremitting application and a courage that never surrendered. Living in a humble home, with scarcely enough money to buy food for his family, he made the fields and woods his laboratory. Bent over on hands and knees, he would spend hours under the scorching sun, following the movements of ants in the grass, watching the maneuvers of beetles in the field, studying the behavior of wasps in their burrows. From sun-up to sun-set he would follow the movements of the insect he was studying, until he could chart its way of life with an accuracy which had never previously been achieved.

When the Minister of Public Education was visiting schools in the neighborhood, he asked to be escorted to the home of Fabre. He found the great naturalist in his overalls, with sleeves rolled up, and his hands red with chemical dye. Hiding his "lobster claws" behind his back, he apologized for his appearance.

Complimenting him on laying bare so many secrets of the insect world, the minister said:

"I will help you. What do you want for your laboratory?"

"Why nothing, M. le Minstre, nothing," replied Fabre. "With a little application, the equipment I have is ample."

"What—nothing! You are unique there. The others overwhelm me with requests. Their laboratories are never well enough supplied. And you, poor as you are, refuse my offer."

Then Fabre told the minister how he made the fields and the woods his laboratory and studied the insects from morning to night. He would go out into the red dawn to watch the resurrection of the silkworm moth in order not to lose the moment when the nymph bursts her swaddling bands. By night he studied the Cione constructing a capsule of goldbeater's skin or the processional caterpillars moving head to tail along their path.

"My heart," he said, "beats with emotion, as I watch my little subjects, ferret out their secrets, and pass hours of oblivion in the happiness of learning."

He would bring his findings to the walnut table "spotted with ink and scarred with knife-cuts, just big enough to hold the inkstand, a halfpenny bottle, and his open notebook." From sixty to ninety, when most men look for repose, Fabre did most of his writing. He toiled over his books with meticulous care.

"As though I had a long future before me," he said at eighty, "I continue my researches into the lives of these little creatures. The outer world scarcely tempts me at all; surrounded by my little family, it is enough for me to go into the woods from time to time, to listen to the fluting of the blackbirds. Away with repose! For him who would spend his life properly there is nothing like work."

He was ninety when a friend broke the news to him that the people of France were going to erect a statue of him in a nearby spot.

"Well, well," he said, "I shall see myself, but shall I recognize myself? I've had so little time to look at myself."

"What inscription do you wish on the statue?"

"One word: *Labor,*" he replied.

Did it take courage to pursue his little subjects in their tortuous and mysterious ways, tracking them down in hole and burrow, working twelve to fifteen hours a day for seventy-five years? Try it and see.

Louis Pasteur

The name which towers most impressively in all medicine is that of Louis Pasteur. Of him alone can it be said that he laid the foundations for several distinct branches of science. He is the founder of physio-chemistry, the father of bacteriology, and the inventor of bio-therapeutics. His whole life is a story of intellectual courage, the courage to assault the foes — ignorance and superstition — which darken the human mind.

He spelled that courage out in a life of unremitting toil, the fruits of which are growing with the passing years. The lodestar of his whole life was work. "Work, work always," was his favorite motto. On his deathbed he turned to the pupils who were keeping their vigil over the master's last hours.

"Where are you?" he said — his hand groped out in the darkness that was closing in upon him — "What are you doing?"

Then he ended with his favorite words: "It is necessary to work."

At the inauguration of the Institut Pasteur in 1888, the famous scientist closed his address with the following words: "Two opposing laws seem to me now in contest. The one, a law of blood and death, opening out each day new modes of destruction, forces nations to be always ready for the battle. The other, the law of peace, work and health, whose only aim is to deliver man from the calamities which beset him. The one seeks violent conquests, the other the relief of mankind. The one places a single life above all victories, the other sacrifices hundreds of thousands of lives to the ambition of a single individual.

"The law of which we are the instruments strives even through the carnage to cure the wounds due to the law of war. Treatment by our antiseptic methods may preserve the lives of thousands of soldiers. Which of these two laws will prevail, God only knows. But of this we may be sure, that science, in obeying the law of humanity, will always labor to enlarge the frontiers of life."

Pasteur's work in developing vaccines, which give immunity from infectious diseases, has saved the lives of hundreds of thousands of human beings. His discoveries practically eliminated the recurring epidemics of chicken cholera and anthrax, a scourge fatal to cattle. Thomas H. Huxley estimated that the monetary value of his discoveries in these fields of animal husbandry was sufficient to cover the whole cost of the war indemnity paid by France to Germany in 1870. In every country of the world human lives are being rescued daily from the fangs of deadly infections by his far-reaching discoveries in bacteriology.

During his lifetime, honors came to him from virtually every civilized country. They did not impair, however, his childlike humility. His faith in God was absolute.

"The more I know," he wrote in a letter to his children, "the more nearly is my faith that of the Breton peasant. Could I but know all, I would have the faith of a Breton peasant's wife."

He saw in the laws of nature, which he deciphered, the

finger writing of God. Over his tomb in the Institut Pasteur are inscribed the following words from one of his addresses, wherein he summarizes his philosophy of life:

"Happy the man who bears within him a divinity, an ideal of beauty, and obeys it; an ideal of art, an ideal of science, an ideal of country, an ideal of the virtues of the Gospel."

Isaac Newton

The intellectual courage which enabled Fabre and Pasteur to concentrate with such vigor upon their search for truth, fighting off for long periods the claims of the body for food and rest, is evident also in the life of Sir Isaac Newton. When he was absorbed in his problems of mathematical physics, the great discoverer of the law of gravitation would work with unremitting application over such long periods as to cause his friends to worry over his health. His man servant reports that when his master was thus preoccupied, he would quietly open the little window in the door of Newton's study and insert the tray of food. When he would come back in the evening with some additional food, he would open the window only to see his previous tray still untouched.

All day long his master was laboring over his desk, working out the principle which holds every particle of the universe, from a grain of sand to the farthest star, in the marvelous network of universal law. This would continue for weeks at a time. Newton himself reports that there were considerable periods of time when he averaged scarcely one hour of sleep per night. Here is stamina, grit, pluck, fortitude, courage, not of the muscles, but of the mind.

Like Pasteur, Newton was a profoundly religious man, and drew much of his courage and strength from union with God in prayer. Toward the end of his life, after many honors had been showered upon him, a friend remarked: "What a comfort it must be to be able to look back over a life of such epochal achievements. In discovering the law of gravitation, you have laid the foundations for both physics and astronomy. You have pushed back the boundary line of the unknown and have brought new worlds under the reign of law. You have every reason to be proud."

"On the contrary," replied Newton, "I must confess to a feeling of profound humility in the presence of a universe which transcends us at almost every point. I feel like a child who while playing by the seashore has found a few bright colored shells and a few pebbles while the whole vast ocean of truth stretches out almost untouched and unexplored before my eager fingers."

Upon his tomb we might well carve the following tribute to a courageous and reverent soul:

For his was not the cold philosophy
Which, finding Law throughout the universe,
Believes the world drives on beneath the curse
Of soulless Force and blind Necessity;
But, reading still above the unfolded Law,
Love's revelation touched his soul with awe.

Carrel and Millikan

Courage, reverence, and humility walk hand in hand.

They constitute the trinity of lovely virtues which distinguish the soldier in the kingdom of the mind who goes forth like Beowulf to slay the dragons of ignorance and superstition.

Most of my life has been spent in close association with scientists at great universities in America and in Europe. I have yet to meet a first-class scientist in whose character the disinterested search for truth was not accompanied by the spirit of reverence and humility. It had the honor of conferring the Cardinal Newman Award upon two of the outstanding winners of the Nobel Prize — Dr. Alexis Carrel for his discoveries in medicine, and Robert Andrews Millikan for his discoveries in nuclear physics. Honors have come to them from many countries, but they have not lessened the sense of reverence and humility which characterize the writings, the speech and the attitude of these two men. A close view of them only enhanced my admiration of their simplicity and humility. With tireless courage, they search for the finger writing of God's laws in the world of the infinitesimally small and in that of the well-nigh infinitely large.

Back of the achievements of all these scientists is the story of unflagging industry. Does that involve courage? Try it. You will find discipline of a high order, self-control that no words can adequately describe, and a patience that never wears out, in the ceaseless application of the mind in the quest for truth. Often, it proves elusive and seems to lead only to will-of-the-wisps; there are tantalizing delays which must be endured, puzzles which rack and torture the brain, frustrations which bite into the marrow of one's soul and challenge his mettle. The courageous soul fights on, however, conscious that all he can put forth is his best, and is willing to leave the outcome to God and the future to decide.

Work of that unstinting character, poured out to the overflowing, is the badge of courage and the hallmark of nobility. No one has proclaimed the gospel of work with greater vigor or persistence than Thomas Carlyle. "Hang your sensibilities," he thundered, "stop your snivelling complaints, and your equally snivelling raptures! Leave off your emotional tomfoolery, and get to WORK like men!"

They do not know at the start, and all their life they can never tell, whether as a result of their work new knowledge, like a new planet, will burst upon their ken. In spite of their ignorance of the objective outcome, however, they carry on to the end. "The true courage of ignorance," observes William Lyon Phelps, "is the courage that faces the unknown outcome with serenity. As has been well said, a calm mind is a victorious mind. And even if the result should be defeat in the practical undertaking, there remains always one victory—the victory over oneself."*

Francis Parkman

The goal of intellectual achievements is always reached by the long road of labor, but that road sometimes is cluttered with the obstacles of physical disabilities and ill health which make the going all the harder. Only intellectual courage of a high order can surmount such a combination

* *The Courage of Ignorance,* New York, E. P. Dutton & Co., p. 59.

of obstacles and convert them into stepping stones to great achievements.

Francis Parkman is a case in point. Even as a boy his health was so delicate that he was obliged to spend several years living out-of-doors at his grandfather's country estate. His frequent journeys into the wilderness engendered a fascination for the forest and helped to decide his life work. This was to be the history of the American conflict between France and Great Britain—a conflict which took place to a great extent in the wilderness of the New World. This theme would enable him to write "the history of the American forest; for this was the light in which I regarded it. My theme fascinated me, and I was haunted with wilderness images day and night."

Before he could complete his studies at Harvard, however, his health broke. After a slow convalescence, he resumed his studies and graduated with honors. To prepare himself properly for his self-appointed task of writing about the wilderness in its gloom and vastness, as well as about its ancient dusky warriors, Parkman lived among them. He shared their hardships and endured their rude and primitive life for many months.

When he began writing *The Conspiracy of Pontiac,* he experienced another relapse; he suffered from nervous exhaustion, aggravated by eye trouble which made it impossible for him to keep his eyes open except in a dark room. This two-fold obstacle would seem sufficient to write *finis* upon his undertaking, foredooming it to failure—but Parkman refused to quit. Against these terrific handicaps he struggled with characteristic courage and fortitude. He invented an apparatus which so supported his hand that he could write legibly with closed eyes. While books and documents were read aloud to him, he made notes while his eyes were shut, and mastered the material with remarkable accuracy. So weak was he, however, that he was only able to work for half an hour a day. Under such appalling difficulties emerged his superb historical monograph in 1851. The American public, however, was not yet sufficiently interested in such a historical theme to give it the reception which it deserved.

No Surrender

Undeterred by this inhospitable reception, Parkman courageously launched himself upon his great work, *France and England in the New World.* This monumental work imposed upon his feeble strength and still feebler eyesight the work of tracing, collecting, arranging and digesting an enormous mass of incongruous material, scattered on both sides of the Atlantic. To make matters worse, a large portion of this material was in handwriting, some of it scarcely legible. It required years of tedious exploration, meticulous copying and arranging. Several journeys to Europe were necessary to locate all the relevant data. Yet Parkman completed his task with a thoroughness approaching finality.

In 1865 the first volume of his monumental work appeared under the title, *Pioneers of France in the New World.* For twenty-seven more years Parkman stuck with Spartan fortitude at his task until the final volume appeared. His volumes, *The Jesuits in North America, LaSalle and the Discovery of the Great West,* and *A Half Century of Conflict,* are monuments not only of scholarship but also of courage that never surrenders.

They disclose the many-sided struggle between the two great European powers for dominance in the New World and afford an authentic picture of the American forest and its Redmen. To the reader who understands the circumstances under which the material was gathered and the books were written, they are not less interesting and significant as revelations of the power of the human will to drive ahead in the face of overwhelming obstacles and to refuse to quit till the goal has been achieved.

His career is a superb illustration of the French critic's definition of a great life—a thought conceived in youth and carried by an indomitable will to complete realization in later years.

Michelangelo

The struggle to achieve beauty in sculpture and in painting calls for intellectual courage which finds expression in infinite pains. To compel the hard granite to respond to the sculptor's concepts of grace of outline and symmetry of figure challenges one's patience and fortitude. To imprison upon the canvas visions of beauty and shades of light and color never seen before upon land or sea demands a concentration of attention and an application which tax the strength and the stamina of the artist. Beauty is the supreme achievement of art. It is the combined product of inspiration and perspiration; the higher the degree of beauty, the greater the mental travail. Wielding one of the most finished styles among the writers of English prose, Cardinal Newman acknowledged that every book he wrote cost him enormous effort and pain.

The visitor to Rome stands in admiration before the great painting of Michelangelo, depicting the story of Genesis from the Creation to the Flood, which adorns the ceiling of the Sistine Chapel. In it there are hundreds of figures, prophets and sibyls, dreaming of the new dispensation to come. This vast array of figures reaches its climax in the forefathers of Christ. The delineation of the human form and face reflects the powers of Michelangelo at their best. Attitudes of unmatched variety and grandeur, countenances of unrivaled expressiveness and power, meet the eye wherever it falls upon the mighty pageant.

Does the spectator ever stop to consider the circumstances under which the painting was executed and the extent of labor involved? After working out a sketch of the vast scene, the master summoned a number of assistant painters from Florence. Unable to interpret Michelangelo's designs in fresco with sufficient freedom or with satisfactory uniformity, they were dismissed. The master then came to grips with the gigantic task—alone. On his back for four and a half years, he toiled on the vast pageant. Hidden in his lonely scaffolding, the great Florentine labored with courage and unwearying patience to mirror in form and color the vision that haunted his mind day and night. The result is a masterpiece that belongs to the ages.

The Last Judgment

Some twenty years later Michelangelo was summoned by Pope Clement to paint the great end wall above the altar in the Sistine Chapel. The master was in his sixtieth year when he began anew to fling the fury of his towering genius into the portrayal of the Last Judgment. Here was a theme that stirred the soul of the gifted painter to its very depths. The spiritual heir of Dante, with the vivid faith of the Middle Ages lighting up every corner of the mighty drama, the great Florentine was kindled into incandescence as the figures of pope, cardinal, priest, merchant, prince, pauper and all the other types of mankind appear for weal or woe at the great Assizes. God, he knew, was no respecter of person or place, and he depicts stern justice falling like thunderbolts upon the heads of the mighty in Church and State.

For seven years he labored upon his stirring drama. When finally the brush dropped from his exhausted hand, he looked up at the masterpiece that was destined to become the most famous single painting in the world. Like the previous one, this was executed in answer to imperative demands, and in the face of Michelangelo's own conviction that sculpture and not painting was the field of his greatest power. Courage, grit, stamina and pluck are mirrored in that immortal painting not less clearly than the grandeur and power of a great genius.

As I gazed in rapt admiration at the mighty painting, there came to my mind the words of J. M. Barrie: "Sometimes beauty boils over and then spirits are abroad." For the spectator can feel and almost see the spirits of the other world as they hasten to and fro, in the execution of the divine decrees of judgment, consigning some to the joys of Heaven, and other, alas! to the nether world. The great poetry of Dante, with its vivid imagery of Heaven and of Hell, had been flung by the fury of the Florentine's genius into a symphony of vivid color that not only gripped one's eyes but filled one's ears and made his heart echo with the music of mighty issues that stretched from time into the dim regions of eternity.

O. Henry tells of a girl living alone in a big city. In time of temptation, she found her courage mounting as she looked at the picture of the doughty Kitchener and thought of the foes he faced with never a thought of surrender. The person engaged in scholarly work, who finds his courage faltering, will find it mounting, too, as he thinks of the mighty Florentine sticking at his post of duty till the last stroke is painted or the last light touch of the chisel falls caressingly upon the sculptured marble.

A Torch for All

Achieving world eminence in sculpture, painting, architecture, and distinction in poetry, working away until his death on the threshold of his ninetieth birthday, Michelangelo has written an epic of courage in the annals of art. In the orchestration of the powers of his gifted mind, one catches ever and anon the overtones from the iron chord of courage vibrating in his soul. His sculptured figures, David and Moses, no less than the painting of the scenes from Genesis and the Last Judgment, are monuments of intellectual courage that mobilized all the latent powers of his nature till they reached the full torrent of his towering genius which flung open the doors of beauty in painting and in sculpture for all the world to gaze upon and admire. In burning up his genius in unremitting labor, he has become a torch for all mankind. His philosophy of life may be thus epitomized;

> *Heaven doth with us as we with torches do*
> *Not light them for themselves.*

The warfare which the scholar must wage is against the ignorance, intolerance, and stupidity of man. That is a war which knows no ending; it is waged for the most part in the lonely solitude of the thinker's cell. Upon his banner might well be inscribed the words which expressed the guiding principle of Thomas Jefferson's life, as they do of every scholar: "I have sworn upon the altar of God eternal hostility against every form of tyranny over the mind of man."

Human nature shrinks from loneliness. Without solitude, however, the depth of thought which marks a true scholar is seldom, if ever, achieved. Courage is required to face that black gulf of isolation, day after day. "Only when you have worked alone," observed the late Justice Oliver Wendell Holmes, "when you have felt around you a black gulf of solitude more isolating than that which surrounds the dying man, and in hope and in despair have trusted to your own unshaken will — then only will you have achieved. Thus only can you gain the secret isolated joy of the thinker, who knows that, a hundred years after he is dead and forgotten, men who never heard of him will be moving to the measure of his thought — the subtle rapture of a postponed power, which the world knows not because it has no external trappings, but which to his prophetic vision is more real than that which commands an army."

Behind every discovery in science and the achievement of every masterpiece in literature and in art is the story of intellectual courage which scorned rest or compromise till the truth was emancipated or beauty was enthroned before the eyes of men.

Summary

Intellectual courage is necessary for the solution of every important problem. It is needed not only by the artist, the scholar, the scientist, but also by every one of us in meeting the problems which each day is likely to bring to us. There are two important steps in its atttainment. The first is to turn and confront the problem, to study it carefully, to analyze it and then to act on the insight which always issues from such sustained thought and study. When such light has been secured on the method of attacking the problem, there is time then—and only then—for the second step. That consists in securing a clear vision of the ideal which will supply motive power for the all-out mobilization of all our resources.

That ideal may be beauty, truth, goodness, health, happiness, love or any of the other ideals which function in our daily life, thought, and conduct. Without intellectual courage, the individual bogs down under a host of fears and anxieties which paralyze him and fill his soul with dread;

vacillation and uncertainty are his waking companions and nightmares disturb his sleep. Fortunate and happy indeed is the individual who acquires early in life the habit of intellectual courage. Neither loneliness nor blackness of night will have any dread for him.

RULE 5. *Turn and confront the problem that is disturbing you; study it carefully, analyze its conflicting values and then decide on the value which you think is most worthwhile. Concentrate on that value and you will find that it will provide motive power for the courageous mobilization of all your powers to achieve your goal.*

Reflect upon the instances of courage cited in this chapter and wait until tomorrow to read the next chapter.

CHAPTER SIX

COURAGE IN POLITICS

Moral courage is a virtue of higher cast and nobler origin than physical. It springs from a consciousness of virtue, and renders a man, in the pursuit of right, superior to the fear of reproach, opposition, or contempt.

— S. G. Goodrich

EVERY CITIZEN HAS NEED *of civic courage. It is especially needed in a democracy where the calibre of the government reflects the intelligence and moral character of the voters. They are called upon to choose representatives in the national, state, county and city administrations. If any of those administrations is honeycombed with graft, racketeering and corruption, it is due to the failure of the voters to elect competent and honest officials.*

Cynics are fond of deriding a democracy as the government of the indifferent by the unscrupulous. The records of many of our city administrations show how apt is that description: the tie-up of politics with crime is so notorious as to make America one of the most lawless nations in the world. Al Capone and Lucky Luciano are but the symbols of the racketeering that infests virtually every large city, mulcting the taxpayers of millions of dollars annually. The most serious threat to our democratic form of government stems not from a foreign foe but from the failure of citizens to elect competent and honest officials; basically, the defect is one of moral cowardice.

How can civic courage be developed? Like other forms of courage, this, too, requires eyes and a will. The first step is for the citizen to face the situation frankly, to study the record of the candidates and to decide on the basis of objective evidence who the best qualified candidates are. The study should be made with care and a scrupulous resistance to unworthy inducements — to vote for a candidate because he is of the same lodge, faith, or racial extraction. These specious appeals should be spurned as totally unworthy of a citizen whose dominant consideration should be the welfare of the community and not the enrichment of a candidate.

The second step is to make the ideal of undivided loyalty to the public interest the controlling motive in all voting. By reflecting upon the good results which will accrue from acting upon such a motive, that motive becomes a psychologically stronger and ultimately pulls the trigger of action. It is a profound truth of psychology that a motive grows in power and influence in proportion to the degree in which the spotlight of attention is focused upon the beneficial effects which flow from its adoption and the harm which follows its rejection.

Such, then, is the twofold technique which will enable an individual to acquire one of the most important virtues in a democracy — the virtue of political honesty, which is but another name for civic courage. The individual who is elected to public office will find it possible to strengthen his intention to discharge faithfully the duties of his office by occasional reflections upon the ideal which should activate all his conduct—undivided loyalty and devotion to the public weal. Through such meditations the ideal will be a functional one, which is but another way of saying that it becomes the motivating force of moral conduct.

Moral Courage

The highest form of courage is moral courage. It is the most difficult of all. It is the capacity to go against the social pressure of a group, to withstand the clamorous tyranny of the mob, out of loyalty to one's convictions. This form of courage moves in the realm of ideas. It runs the gamut of the scorn, ridicule and abuse of the crowd. That which men crave most deeply is the applause and admiration of the public; most people would face physical danger and even death before they would face the shame and scorn of public opinion. Warden Lawes, with his long experience at Sing Sing, has said that this is true even of hardened criminals, who cringe and smart before the scorn of their fellow inmates.

The force of public opinion is therefore most powerful in fashioning social conduct; it will whip into line virtually every citizen of a nation. When aroused and articulate, it is immensely more powerful than any law on a statute book. In fact, any law which is not anchored in public opinion will not long survive.

There are times, however, when an individual sincerely believes public opinion is wrong. Here he must choose between following the verdict of the crowd and the dictate of conscience. To follow the latter requires that he run the gamut of public condemnation and obloquy: a form of punishment from which many a person with abundant physical courage will shrink and flee. Because this punishment bites into the very marrow of the ego as reflected in the public eye, most people find it the most bitter and the most intolerable of all.

How often has one heard a person say: "I would rather take a beating than do that." Why? Because such a deed would bring him not a physical beating, but the scourging of social disapproval and, therefore, greater pain.

The central topic of our discussion here is courage in politics. With a view of making the difference between physical and moral courage crystal clear, however, we shall first take an illustration from a non-political field.

Gene Tunney has given many an exhibition of physical gameness. Twice he faced the murderous blows of the Manassa Mauler in the squared ring and lifted the heavyweight crown from one of the greatest fighters that the game has ever known. But, one night in a Midwestern city, Tunney faced a still more formidable foe. He was the guest of honor at a stag banquet; following it, the entertainment committee had arranged for a floor show. To Tunney's surprise, it featured a couple of virtually nude female dancers.

Such an exhibition was offensive to Tunney's moral code. What was he to do? To arise and leave would be flying in the face of the social pressure. Here was a case calling not for physical gameness, but for moral courage. Tunney proved equal to it. Arising from his seat at the speakers' table, he said: "Gentlemen, I don't care for this type of exhibition. I find it indecent and offensive. You'll have to excuse me." He walked quickly from the room. Others followed. In my opinion, this was the bravest fight that Gene Tunney ever fought and won — a victory of unflinching moral courage.

A Senate Scene

Early in the spring of 1917, I listened to the debates which raged in the Senate over America's entrance into World War I. By that time the country had been inundated with tidal waves of propaganda for war. Throughout the country the press had worked up the war spirit, so that it had become fashionable and patriotic to shout for war and to assail all speakers who asked the nation to stay out of the raging volcanoes of European hatreds. The Eastern newspapers had been particularly bellicose and had inflamed that section of the country with the war fever.

I remember listening one afternoon to a two-hour address by Senator Stone of Missouri. He pleaded for America to use her good offices to bring the warring leaders to the peace table, but to abstain from throwing her young men into the fires of European enmities and never-dying hatreds. Whether one agrees or disagrees with the stand the Senator took, I think all must admit it was one which required great moral courage. As chairman of the Foreign Relations Committee, he was under terrific pressure to reflect the policy of the Wilson Administration then pressing vigorously for war.

The great majority of the Senate by that time had been won over to the war policy. The crowds in the galleries, inflamed with the passions of war, contrary to all the rules broke out repeatedly in hisses when the Senator pleaded for abstinence from European quarrels and for some regard for the lives of our own young men. Newspapers called him a "Hun sympathizer" and applied to him other labels which were chiefly libels. Atrocity stories, which had been manufactured in offices set up for that purpose, had swept the country and instilled the war spirit into a people who normally wish only to live in peace and good will with all nations.

I have never been able to forget the sight of Senator Stone facing the hostility of the galleries, the displeasure of the majority of his colleagues, and the wrath of the administration leaders to follow the voice of his conscience and plead for abstinence from the interminable squabbles of the Old World. Along with him stood LaFollette, O'Gorman, Norris, Reed and a few others, all of whom President Wilson branded as the "twelve wilful men" because they dared to defy his demand for war.

"Country above Party"

Some twenty years later, I had occasion to confer upon Senator George Norris the Cardinal Newman Award for distinguished public service. Then I learned at first hand of what he had to face in the way of public criticism because of his vote. When he went back to Nebraska to give an account of his vote to his constituents, he found it impossible to get a single prominent citizen to preside at the meeting. No one wished to be tarred with the stigma of association with a man who had voted to keep out of the blood baths of Europe.

That had become not only unpatriotic, but closely akin to treason. Nevertheless, George Norris faced that crowd with a clear conscience, which is the true source of moral courage.

There is something infectious about courage, and before Norris left that crowded hall, he had won over the crowd from hostility to applause for his own fearless obedience to the deepest convictions of his conscience.

I can think of few men in public life who have shown in season and out of season such moral courage as Senator Norris. Coming to see early in his public career that blind obedience to the behests of the bosses within one's political party was inconsistent with the best interests of the country, Norris declared his intention to follow his own conscience.

"I was elected," he once said, "to serve my country, not the interests of any political party."

Though elected originally on the Republican ticket, Norris did not hestitate to support a measure introduced by a Democrat, if he thought it was really a good measure. Neither did he hestitate to campaign for a Democratic candidate when he was convinced that he was a better public servant than the individual proposed by his own party. He afforded the country the first spectacle of a United States Senator, elected originally on the Republican ticket, campaigning not only in his own state, but in others as well, for the Democratic candidate for the Presidency.

He had come to look upon these party labels as virtually

meaningless; he demanded that the voters look beneath these tags and inspect the real goods. He had been disgusted in Washington with innumerable instances of alleged public servants placing the interests of their party before their country.

"Young Man, If . . ."

Early in his career in the House of Representatives an incident had occurred which showed him the folly of traipsing along blindly with his party. A Democratic leader had introduced a resolution to adjourn Congress on the morrow out of respect for Washington's birthday. Whereupon, a Republican leader assailed him and his party as loafers and urged that the best way to pay tribute to the Father of our country was by holding the usual session. Norris thought the resolution introduced by the Democratic leader entirely reasonable and voted for it.

That evening in the cloak room a Republican leader took Norris to task for not voting with his party.

"Young man," he said, "if you want to stay long in this House, you'll have to vote as your party leader tells you. The cemetery is full of political corpses who failed to obey orders."

A slow anger began to kindle in the breast of Norris. Later that evening, he found that exactly the reverse of the action in the House had taken place in the Senate. A Republican had moved to adjourn for the morrow, while a Democrat had opposed. The vote was along the usual party lines.

"If blind obedience to party orders leads to such contradiction in small matters," Norris reflected, "why will it not produce the same glaring inconsitency and folly in important matters?" From then on, for forty years of public service, Norris followed through thick and thin the voice of his own conscience.

It was of no consequence to him whether the measure bore the Democratic label or that of the G.O.P. What alone concerned him were the merits of the measure. Was it for the best interests of the country as a whole? This became the touchstone by which he was able to separate the chaff from the wheat.

His party leaders raged and stormed. They sought to knife him and throw his carcass to the political wolves eager for his blood. They even resorted to the dishonest trick of placing on the ballot the name of an obscure Nebraska groceryman, also named George W. Norris, thinking they would thereby confuse voters and by this form of subtle fraud have the Senator counted out. But the citizens of Nebraska, like those of every state, admire courage and place a high premium on unflinching honesty. For some forty years they returned Norris to Washington, honoring him with one of the longest tenures of high office in our nation's history.

Norris' example infected others. In consequence, we have today a growing number of members of Congress who are not afraid to put the welfare of the nation above that of party. In the continued growth of this body lies the hope of the advancement of the well-being and prosperity of the American people. Along with the elder Robert

LaFollette in pioneering in this field stands George W. Norris, whose name has become a symbol of courage in the field of politics.

The Way of the Politician

Moral courage is particularly needed in political life. Here, the traditional policy has been to do the expedient, the opportune thing. Politicians are concerned chiefly with the immediate consequences of their actions — how the voters react — not with the long-term consequences of a measure. The gods of the politician are Expediency and Opportunism: before these idols they worship and are willing to sell their souls. The consequence is that politics has become the breeding ground of moral timidity, if not of cowardice.

The prevailing custom is to straddle issues, to agree with everyone and to differ with no one, even though constituents want contradictory policies to be pursued. The past master in politics has learned the art of blowing hot and cold at the same time. The yardstick of all measures is "a count of the noses." "It is *well* to know the truth and speak it," runs an Oriental proverb, "but it is *better* to know the truth and speak about the palm trees." While this might be a prudent policy to follow in a country ruled by a ruthless despot, it should have no place in a democracy where free discussion and the voicing of one's honest convictions are of the very essence.

Here, the straddling propensity, the fawning spirit, the non-committal attitude, the time-serving disposition render difficult, if not impossible, the development of honest and courageous leadership in public life. By lulling the voters into somnolence about public issues, they undermine good citizenship. Thus does democracy, so glorious in theory, tend in practice to become a government of the indifferent by the unscrupulous.

The tendency among typical politicians who seldom, if ever, want "to stand and be counted" is to shelve controversial questions as speedily as possible or to cloak them with shirking reticence. When a live issue comes to the fore, the dominant policy is to

. . . shut the door
With mystery before and reticence behind.

"Addition, Division, Silence"

Political diplomacy has become the art of using words to say as little as possible. One of its typical representatives, Talleyrand, went so far as to say that language was made to conceal thought. This attitude doesn't make for honesty; neither does it make for courage. It makes for a postponement of the issue, a shying away from facts, an ostrich habit of burying one's head in the sand, and, as a wag has impishly added, inviting by one's posture what's coming to him.

A person of wide experience in city administration tells me that it is this conspiracy of silence, this hush-up policy, this "let matters well enough, alone" procedure which makes possible the widespread graft and corruption existing today. "There are hundreds, and even thousands of towns and cities," he said, "where slot-machines and other gambling devices are operating wide open. The rake-off runs each year into the millions. It is often split four ways, to each of the leading public officials — the mayor, the state's attorney, the sheriff, and the chief of police—charged with the enforcement of the laws against such gambling. Sometimes, the newspaper publisher is also given a slice for keeping silent. These persons never collect in person. They have their agents pick up each month their share of the slush fund for them."

Hundreds of thousands of citizens know this is going on. Yet, rare indeed is the individual who so much as says "boo" about the great American game of "addition, division and silence." A little bit of moral courage would sever with the promptness of a razor's stroke the widespread tie-up of politics with organized gambling and with that still more malignant enemy — commercialized vice. Legislature can legislate, aldermen can pass ordinances, and clergymen can exhort, till the cows come home, but the tie-up of politics with crime will continue until men with moral courage arise to blast the conspiracy of silence and to turn on the light by the fearless proclamation of the facts.

Fighting Al Capone

I listened to the story told to my students by George E. Q. Johnson, when as federal District Attorney of Chicago, he was seeking to secure the conviction of the notorious gangster, Al Capone. He and his fellow thugs had gained the ascendancy in Chicago in bootlegging which had mushroomed overnight into a fifty million-dollar racket. He had already "muscled" into control of a number of labor unions; his syndicate was levying a tax upon merchants for "protection." Scarcely a week passed without some one being murdered, frequently under particularly ghastly circumstances, as a result of his widespread operations.

Persons who were shot, but did not die, were almost invariably too afraid to reveal the name of the would-be murderer. Witnesses were called in, only to experience a sudden attack of forgetfulness; other witnesses disappeared before the case came to court. When word got out that a witness was talking, he would suddenly be killed. Even hospitals were invaded, and injured victims were finished off to keep them from talking.

The citizens seemed cowed: vice, crime and murder were rampant. Gangsters were becoming millionaires, with winter homes in Florida; oriental rugs graced their palaces; gold knobs adorned their doors. Capone & Company appeared to have law and order by the throat, and were laughing in unholy glee.

"The greatest difficulty that I experienced in prosecuting that case," said Johnson, "was in trying to get witnesses to testify. Time after time we would bring witnesses to my office only to find them lacking courage to testify or to give us the slightest help. We would promise them police protection. But, even then, we rarely found a man who had courage enough to put in his appearance on the witness stand. They wanted protection as citizens, but they were unwilling to give the testimony which would have removed the boss of the criminals from circulation and enabled us to smash his ring."

"We Needed Courage"

"If ever there was a need for courage, it was in the lawless period when we were fighting an uphill fight against the most formidable organization of criminals and gangsters that ever spewed horror and death upon the citizens of Chicago. We needed men and women who had courage to talk out in the court to enable us to put this desperate criminal under lock and key."

Johnson and his associates finally secured a conviction —on grounds of income tax law violation—and had Capone sentenced to Alcatraz. Before achieving that, however, they found it necessary to place prospective witnesses in a vessel out on Lake Michigan to keep them from fleeing on the wings of fear.

The simple fact is that the enormous toll, running each year into billions, taken from the pockets of the taxpayers, through widespread graft and corruption, through the tie-up of politics and commercialized vice, through racketeering and crime, is chiefly traceable to the lack of moral courage on the part of all those charged with the enforcement of law. Sharing in that culpability is the vast legion of citizens who know of crookedness in high places and in low, but who do not say a word or lift a finger to end the disgrace. This is the malady which is making the administration of our cities reel and stagger like a drunken man. It is the carcinoma of American democracy, a cancer which clamors for eradication by the scalpel of moral courage.

Opportunism and expediency beget the politicians; courage begets the statesman. Between the two, there is a world of difference. The former's avocation is holding his ear to the ground. The latter holds his head erect, his eyes forward; he comes to grips with a problem and seeks a solution in the light of reason and experience. Public officials would do well to heed the truth which Lincoln made the guiding principle of his life. "I am not bound to win," he said, "but I am bound to be true. I am not bound to succeed, but I am bound to live up to the light I have. I must stand with anybody that stands right, stand with him while he is right, and part with him when he goes wrong."

Senator Johnson Replies

Senator Hiram Johnson won the admiration of friend and foe by the courage he displayed in standing by his convictions. A delegation once called upon the Senator and informed him that they represented seventy newspaper editors in California who would actively oppose his re-election unless he changed his views on a certain measure. In the face of such formidable and articulate opposition, most candidates would have flopped over, or at least would have sought to conciliate them with honeyed words.

Not Hiram Johnson. "Go and tell those editors," replied the Senator, "that if seventy times seventy editors oppose me, I will stand by my convictions." The electorate perceived his courage, flocked to his standard, and re-elected him by an overwhelming majority. He enjoyed the unique distinction of being nominated for the Senate by both the Republican and Democratic parties. As in the case of Senator Norris, the electorate has shown its admiration for courage and honesty by rewarding Senator Johnson with an unusually long tenure of high public office.

While it is true that courage may exist without practical wisdom, there is a strong presumption that they go together. "The possession of habitual courage," observes Coventry Patmore, "implies that a man understands what he is doing and whither he is going." Moreover, the collapse of courage is not infrequently followed by failure of insight and the breakdown of judgment. People lose the power of perceiving the truth when they lose the habit of obeying it. Nature rebels against the dichotomy that results from seeing the truth and failing to obey it. If the practice is long indulged, nature achieves a unity, even though it be a pathological one, by dulling the vision or desensitizing the inner ear of conscience. Here is the psychological genesis of the process of rationalization, wherein one uses his reason to fabricate arguments to justify his moral deliquency. Herein is perceived likewise the inner deformation which results from the habitual failure of moral courage — the taint of nature's punishment.

When John Stuart Mill was running for Parliament, his opponent appeared on the platform and taunted him with a quotation from one of his books. Therein Mills had expressed his conviction that the judgement of the masses could not be trusted in complex and involved questions demanding training in weighing the evidence pro and con. Thinking that he had Mill in a tight spot where an admission would incur the disfavor of the crowd, he asked:

"Mr. Mill, did you, or did you not, make that statement reflecting on the judgment of the people?"

"I did," replied Mill, "and I stand by it now."

Whereupon, the crowd broke in with thunderous applause. Even though the statement was not complimentary to them, they admired the fearless honesty of the man who made it, and they were not slow to show it.

Dewey Declares War

During the twenty-two years in which I was the Director of the Newman Foundation at the University of Illinois, I was privileged to bring many eminent persons to the University, to receive at a public convocation The Cardinal Newman Award for distinguished contributions to science, literature, art or public service. Of all those illustrious personages, I think the general student body showed probably the greatest enthusiasm and the most rapturous acclaim for Thomas E. Dewey, then District Attorney of New York City. Perhaps his youthfulness had something to do with it, for youth appeals to youth and captures their imagination most readily. But probably the factor which, more than any other, accounted for the spontaneous and tumultuous acclaim accorded him wherever he appeared upon the campus was that in the eyes of the students he was a symbol of youthful courage.

He had thrown himself into a life and death struggle with the gangsters and gorillas who, under "Lucky" Luciano and other leaders, had a nation's metropolis by the throat. Repeated attempts to place these gangsters, fattening on the enormous rake-off from organized gambling and commercialized vice, had fizzled out ignominiously. As in Chicago under "Scarface" Al Capone, witnesses were intimidated or killed; a few minor thugs took the rap, while the overlords grew more arrogant and insolent every day.

Throwing the gauntlet down to these murderous gorillas, the youthful district attorney asked no quarter and gave none. He brought a marvelous efficiency into the methods of collecting evidence, gaining the confidence of witnesses and protecting them. Then he proceeded to bear down with merciless precision and strangling evidence upon the overlords grown fat and sleek in the purchased immunity which they had so long enjoyed.

With the whole nation watching, this youthful gladiator hurled the thunderbolts of public indignation into the inner circles and threw the noose of long-delayed justice around the necks of the vice moguls. Syndicates which reached out their grasping fingers into thousands of dens to collect the lion's share of the loot, from the prostitutes, panderers, gamblers and racketeers, began to crumble. The luck of "Lucky" Luciano began to wane; shyster lawyers, splitting the spoils with the vice overlords, found New York too hot for comfort. The Augean stables of the metropolis, reeking with the filth of corruption, graft, and commercialized vice and crime, which had become a stench in the nostrils of the nation, got such a cleansing as they had never received in their history.

The Need Today

The overlords were either executed or put beind the bars; the syndicates were broken up, their captains jailed; the citizens breathed freely again. The city was able once more to call its soul its own — without paying tribute to

"Lucky" Luciano or his mobsters. So deep was the admiration of the people of the nation for a difficult job, done with courage, ability and honesty, that soon the name of Thomas E. Dewey, despite his exceeding youthfulness, began to lead in the straw votes throughout the country, as a presidential candidate.

It was shortly after winning his fight against the vice moguls of New York that Dewey came to the campus. No dignitary of State or Church, however eminent he might be, would have evoked the spontaneous outpouring of admiration, enthusiasm and affection from the student body which was showered upon this brave and modest young man. In the long history of the University, no visitor, I am certain, ever received an acclaim that came so close to idolatry as that which was accorded Thomas E. Dewey. He established a pattern of efficiency for every such office in the country. More than that: he endued that office with the spirit of uncompromising courage.

Why should not every incumbent in such an office, I have often wondered, follow a pattern and emulate a spirit which brought such shining victory in a locale where defeat was traditional? It brings rich returns in the administration of justice, in the protection of the community from gangsters, and in the gratitude of the people. With crime growing by leaps and bounds, the crying need in America today is for officials who have the courage to carry the war to gangsters, grafters, racketeers, and criminals, and to pursue them without ceasing till the last one is securely behind the bars. Theirs will be the victory of moral courage over slinking cowardice — the invariable mark of the criminal.

A Task for All

This is not, however, the job of public officials alone: it is the task of all the people — the electorate and officials working shoulder to shoulder. Public servants need the backing of public opinion, they need the whole-hearted cooperation of every man, woman and child, to secure the observance of all the laws of a community. Too often, in the past, citizens failed to go in sufficient numbers to the polls to elect capable and conscientious candidates: too often they regarded their work as done when they cast their ballot. That attitude of crass indifference, must be replaced by one of ceaseless vigilance for the public good.

How many so-called good people regard politics as a dirty business, with which they disdain to soil their white kid gloves. They have time for bridge and other social pastimes. But for the important business of electing capable public servants they have no time. This is a form of civic cowardice that approaches treason. Such careless and indifferent citizens are not only slackers, but criminals, for to their apathy is traceable in the last analysis the election of unqualified officials and the consequent failure to enforce the law.

American boys have shed their blood in foreign lands for the preservation of the ideals of democracy, for the safeguarding of the American way of life. Have we kept faith with them? Have we fought with courage and determination to safeguard the right of the ballot for all? What about the ten million Negro citizens whom we asked to go abroad to fight for the freedom of people in distant lands, when suffrage is denied to the majority of them in the

Southern states? Such a contradiction is the breeding ground of hatred, injustice and crime.

"Go out into foreign lands," we told our soldiers, "and fight for the freedom from want for the Europeans . . . the Africans . . . the Asiatics . . ." while here at home millions of our people are living in squalid poverty. No less an authority than the President of the United States has declared that a third of our people are living below the standard of American life. In recent years the richest one-tenth of one per cent of American families was getting an income equal to that of 42 per cent at the other end of the scales. This means that 36,000 wealthy families received as much as 11,653,000 poor families. All the time we prate of "democracy . . . liberty . . . and equality." The stark facts make these words look like ghosts in the night.

The fight for social justice, for civic decency, and for the realization of the ideals of democracy challenges the courage and the fortitude of all our citizens. Here is a battle that must be fought not with bombing planes and submarines, but with intelligence, patience, and perseverance. In the winning of that battle to make the ideals of democracy living realities throughout the length and breadth of America, we shall need a courage that is unsurpassed.

Summary

Every individual should develop the habit of civic courage, so necessary in a democracy. Without it, democracy becomes the rule of the indifferent by the unscrupulous. The tie-up of politics with gamblers, racketeers and criminals is responsible for the graft and corruption so widespread in our cities. This alliance can be broken by the action of our citizens in electing competent and honest officials and in backing up their efforts to provide a clean and efficient administration.

The individual develops civic courage through a twofold procedure: (1) Study carefully the record of all candidates to determine the best qualified not on the basis of blind partisanship or racial or religious clannishness but of objective evidence; (2) Make the ideal of promoting the public weal the controlling motive in casting your ballot. You can make that ideal the prevailing motive by reflecting upon the benefits that flow to you and to all society from pursuing that ideal with persistence and determination. Only in this way does an individual share in the teamwork of voter and public official, without which democracy becomes a sham and a delusion.

RULE 6. *Develop political courage by voting for the best candidate. Form the habit of investigating the qualifications of candidates for public office and vote for the best qualified, regardless of their party, religious affiliation or racial extraction, in spite of inducements or pressure to vote otherwise; make the public welfare the dominant consideration in all your political actions and thus you develop the civic conscience and political courage without which a democracy cannot long endure.*

Reflect upon the instances of courage cited in this chapter and wait until tomorrow to read the next chapter.

CHAPTER SEVEN

FOOLS FOR GOD

We are fools for Christ's sake.

— Paul, *I Cor.* 4:10

An individual is a citizen of a particular country and is normally devoted to its welfare. He is also a citizen of the world and should be devoted to the welfare of all mankind; in this day of speedy transportation, lightning-like communication and atom bombs, this is truer than ever before; human society stands or falls together. Civilization progresses and becomes more secure largely in proportion as an increasing number of people can truthfully say: "My country is the world. My countryman are all mankind."

To act upon that principle, courage is needed. It is a form of moral courage that springs from the clear realization of the basic unity of mankind — that God is our Father and we are all brothers. For the development of this kind of courage, cosmic and humanitarian in character, it is necessary to reflect upon two fundamental truths:

(1) *The personality of each individual possesses a dignity and a sanctity which transcends all earthly values; because man is made in the image and likeness of God, his personality mirrors a divine being. We must see the lineaments of the face of Christ in the countenance of every human creature, regardless of race or creed.*

(2) *Whatsoever we do unto any person is to be viewed as being done unto God Himself. "Amen I say to you," said Jesus, "as long as you did it to one of these my least brethren, you did it to me."*

The implications of these two germinal truths are as tremendous as they are far-reaching; the narrow borderlines of class, country and race are extended so as to embrace all mankind. My brother is the impoverished East Indian ten thousand miles away; the kindness I extend to him in his hour of need is a kindness extended unto Christ. Herein are the seeds of human brotherhood from which alone can blossom the precious fruit of international friendship and world peace. To strive to build world peace upon any other basis is to build it upon shifting sand. What is desperately needed to heal a wounded and aching world today is an increasing number of people who have the courage to translate Christ's ideal into practice — to become fools for God and servants to all mankind.

A Different Courage

We are accustomed to think of courage as a martial virtue. We think of it as an attribute of warriors, having its rendezvous on the field of battle. A closer investigation will disclose, however, that it rests like a crown upon the brow of men and women who spend themselves in struggling for the underprivileged, the downtrodden and the oppressed, and who walk in the paths of peace. Their courage is different from that of the soldier on the battlefield. The men and women who have broken the chains of slavery, who have lifted the downtrodden from their hovels of degradation, and who have removed the burdens from the bent shoulders of the oppressed, have also been soldiers, but they have been soldiers of peace, of healing, of enlightenment, of charity.

Theirs is the moral courage that enables them to face without flinching the ignorance, stupidities and prejudices of their day, and to conquer these enemies of mankind. Theirs is the quiet, serene courage which springs from the conviction of the righteousness of their cause and enables them to withstand the raillery, the jeering, and the abuse so often hurled upon the apostles of social progress and the benefactors of the race. So often in man's slow upward climb the fagots have been kindled for the saint, the stones gathered for the hero, and the cross raised for the martyr. Theirs has not been a path of velvet, but a path strewn with obstacles which would daunt the faint-hearted.

Yet from these courageous souls, whose minds were lit up by a great vision and whose hearts were set upon a lofty goal, mankind has received more benefactions and blessings than from all the generals whose soldiery shook the earth beneath their martial tread. Let us peer more deeply into the souls of these heroes of mankind, these apostles of human progress, these adventurers for God, and we shall find their courage, though quiet and serene, is admirable indeed and is worthy of our emulation. While their faces are calm and kindly, we shall find that in the music of their soul the iron chord of courage sounds the overtone.

Frederick Ozanam

An organization which now circles the globe with its ministry of charity for the poor and the downtrodden is the Society of St. Vincent de Paul. It had its origin in the vision of a young Frenchman, Frederick Ozanam. A student at the Sorbonne, lonely and reflective, Frederick walked through the poverty-stricken sections of Paris and found his sensitive nature seeking to reach out to aid these people who were living below the level of decent human existence. They lacked proper food, clothing and shelter; Frederick could not efface them from his mind.

He had lodgings at the time with Ampere, who was destined to carve his name deeply in the science of electricity; he was gifted not only with a brilliant mind but also with a generous heart. When Frederick confided to him his solicitude for the poor, Ampere encouraged him and uttered a sentence which Frederick was never to forget: "I should possess everything in the world to make me happy did I possess nothing at all but the happiness of others." It was destined to become the guiding principle of Ozanam's life.

Frederick was attending a meeting of the Societe des Bonnes Etudes, where the members were discussing the past glories of Christianity and the condition of the Church in France. Suddenly a young waiter of Voltairean propensities hurled a bombshell into the meeting by shouting: "What's the use of talking about the past grandeur of the Church? The real question is: What is the Church doing for the poor, the desolate, and the suffering *now?* What is she doing to see that people who are half starving get food? What is she doing to see that people who are half naked get clothing? What is she doing to make life better and happier, not in a distant Hereafter but here and now? Show us your works! By your works you shall be known."

The brief but pointed speech struck home to Ozanam. He could not fail to see that the young waiter had sounded the keynote of the day in France. Devoted member of the Church that he was, he could not close his eyes to the fact that the Church was too closely allied to the monarchy. She had fallen into a cold and apathetic formalism that paid scant attention to the indigent who were drifting farther and farther way from her in their search for a little bit of heaven on this earth.

"Go to the Poor"

Leaving the meeting sadly and thoughtfully with two companions, Ozanam uttered a phrase which was to become the warcry of the new movement: *"Allons aux pauvres!"* — Let us go to the poor! Frederick realized that if religion was to exercise any vital influence upon the society of his day, its adherents would have to go out into the tenements of the impoverished and show them something of the solicitude which throbbed in the heart of Christ. The battle for the soul of France, he perceived, would be fought not in the lecture halls of the University, but in the slums of the cities and in the poverty-ridden tenements of the destitute.

Accordingly, Ozanam organized a group of laymen who were to devote themselves to ministering to those in need. The cardinal principle of the organization was that help and relief were to be given entirely irrespective of religious distinction; the only claim to be recognized was actual need. Furthermore, the ministrations were to be made not by religious but by lay people; this was a bold innovation. Its members were to visit the poor in their homes, to bring them food, clothing, and, when their houses were cold, they were to carry fuel to them.

The first meeting of the organization was held in May, 1833, in the offices of M. Bailey's journal, *La Tribune Catholique.* Six young men assembled. From that small beginning has grown the Society of St. Vincent de Paul, with its hundreds of thousands of members carrying on its works of mercy and charity to the needy and the afflicted throughout the world. The marvelous spirit which animates this society of laymen, based on the brotherhood of Jesus Christ, and dedicated to the ministry of the poor and the needy, is essentially that bequeathed to it by its apostolic young founder.

The Lengthened Shadow

Though Ozanam later became a distinguished professor at the Sorbonne, he never found it beneath his dignity to walk from the lecture halls of this renowned university out into the slums to minister to the poor. It required no small amount of courage, at a time when the intellectuals and the socialites of France disdained personal contact with the ragged underpaid, for Ozanam to walk through the streets of Paris with his arms full of clothing for the destitute. Braving the arched eyebrows of the elite, Ozanam went into the lowest hovels of the unwashed indigent, poured healing oils into the festering sores of the afflicted, and carried fuel to the unheated apartments of shivering tenants. He became in very truth a minister of mercy and an apostle of charity to the most indigent and miserable of Paris's teeming poor.

Something of his solicitude for them and his big-hearted determination to better their lot shone forth in his countenance and burst forth in his lectures. Though not of his faith, Ernest Renan bears witness to the effect of Ozanam's lectures. "I never leave one of his lectures," he stated, "without feeling strengthened, more determined to do something great; more full of courage and hope as regards the future. Ozanam's course of lectures are a continual defense of everything which is most worthy of our admiration. Ozanam, how fond of him we were! What a fine soul!" Such is the testimony of all who came within the spell of this great man and felt the contagion of his quiet courage to better the lot of the destitute, not by paid agents but by his own daily ministrations to their manifold needs.

The work of the hundreds of thousands of members of the society of St. Vincent de Paul encircling the globe today with a rosary of charity bespeak the thoroughness with which Ozanam laid the foundation for his world organization. Every great and lasting achievement is the lengthened shadow of a mighty personality. The Society of St. Vincent de Paul is the lengthened shadow of the quiet courage of Frederick Ozanam to melt the cold formalism of the social and religious life of France under the flame of a compassion for the multitude of God's poor who are destined to be with us always.

Toyohiko Kagawa

The attack upon Pearl Harbor tended to make us think of the Japanese as a race in whom the qualities of treachery and cruelty are indigenous. However well or ill founded is that impression, there is one man in Japan of whom we could never think in terms of such qualities. That man is Toyohiko Kagawa. A convert to Christianity, Kagawa sought with courage and determination to walk in the footsteps of Christ and to follow His divine example at all costs. Amid the raucous voices of inflamed nationalism calling for war, Kagawa consistently pleaded for peace.

He braved the insults of the unthinking masses and the threats of the military class by seeking to stem the growth of the war spirit. His plea was the teaching of Christ that all mankind are brothers, children of the same Almighty Father and that war set brother to slaughtering brother. He was repeatedly thrown into jail, but never changed his tune, or recanted his gospel. America and the cause of peace had no stauncher friend in all Nippon than Toyohiko Kagawa.

Not only did he fight for peace against the rising tide of the war spirit, but he fought for the application of Christ's teaching to the social and industrial life of Japan. Living among the poor, he made their cause his own. Probably more than any man in the Land of the Rising Sun, he has been responsible for lifting the teeming millions of underpaid laborers to a higher plane of life. Through collective bargaining he has greatly increased the miserable pittance previously paid to them, and has enabled them to live with something of the decency to which human beings in every land are entitled. His work in establishing cooperatives to secure for the masses a larger measure of social justice has attracted the attention of economists throughout the world.

Not less impressive than the courage with which he has fought for the rights of the needy and the lowly has been the courage with which he has sought to apply literally the teachings of Christ in his own life—especially the law of an all-embracing love. Witnessing so much dire poverty round about him, he determined to share the lot of the poorest of the poor. He made his home in a little shack, about ten by eight feet, which he shared with a beggar. In spite of the fact that food was scarce, he divided his meagre portion with the indigent.

In this little hut in the slum district of Osobe, Kagawa wrote his radiant songs of Jesus. Here, too, he composed his books which have carried the winsome picture of Christ into the hearts of hundreds of thousands of his countrymen. Even when thrown in jail because of his utterances for peace and for the rights of the poor, he continued to turn out pamphlets and books which became best sellers as quickly as they came off the press.

He Did Not Strike Back

His courage in seeking to apply literally Christ's teaching is illustrated in the following incident. On returning to his hut after having earned a few coins, he was confronted by a bully who demanded his earnings. Knowing that he wanted them to buy liquor, Kagawa refused. Whereupon, the bully rained blow after blow upon his face. He knocked out several of his front teeth and caused the blood to stream from his lips.

Kagawa, however, did not strike back. With a superhuman effort he kept his hands at his side and thought of Christ, buffeted, spat upon, and saying: "If any one strike thee on the right cheek, turn to him the left also." That vision of Christ enabled him to put Christ's injunction into practice.

Amazed at the strange spectacle, the bully fled in dismay. There is something deep down in the heart of man that crumples at the sight of a person who, innocent, defenseless and unafraid, bears the buffetings and blows heaped upon him without striking back. Physical force falls to its knees in awe when confronted with the moral might of the naked human soul. Here was a new type of courage rarely seen before among the Nipponese.

When Kagawa came to America on a lecture tour, he drew some of the largest audiences in recent years. I listened to his moving plea for brotherhood, for social justice for the poor, and, above all, for the practice of Christ's all-embracing law of love, for the courage of Christians to begin to practice what they preach. When I shook hands with him and he smiled, I saw the tell-tale evidence of the bully's beating in the absence of his front teeth.

Toyohiko Kagawa stands as a symbol of courage to put literally into practice Christ's all-embracing law of love, with its injunction not to strike back. I think of him not only as the noblest but also as the most courageous among all the Nipponese—the Christian Gandhi of Japan.

Albert Schweitzer

Back in 1933, I read a book, *Aus Meinem Leben und Denken,* by Albert Schweitzer. It is a sure cure for the blues and for the person who thinks he is overburdened. Even though I did not see eye to eye with its author on theological questions, it brought home to me the story of one of the most versatile and courageous men of our day. His genius is so many-sided that he may be called a modern Leonardo da Vinci. Before he was 30, he had achieved an international reputation as a Biblical scholar, a philosopher, a theologian and a musician. He became the supreme authority on Bach and his greatest living interpreter on the organ.

The concerts he played on the great organs of Europe led him to study their structure with great care; the resulting book on *Organ Building* is the classic in its field. Besides mastering Greek, Latin and Hebrew, he wrote books in German and in French. Students from all parts of Germany flocked to his lectures at the University of Strassburg. Clearly, his star seemed destined to shine with ever-increasing brilliance in the academic firmament of the world.

Then occurred an incident which changed the whole course of his life. He saw the figure of a Negro on a monument in the Colmar market place. It stirred him deeply. The image of the black man in all his utter helplessness continued to haunt him. He read about the plight of the natives in the French Congo. The report of the missionaries told of natives suffering from elephantiasis, sleeping sickness, black fever and a host of diseases which made their lot miserable in the extreme. While we are preaching to them about religion, ran the account, they are suffering and dying from physical maladies, about which we can do nothing.

It brought both a question and a challenge to Schweitzer. Am I to continue to preach about Jesus and His teachings or am I brave enough to try and apply them to these people and bring them the relief they so sorely need? It was easy to preach about Jesus' law of love and mercy. To practice it, however, was more difficult. To bring them the succor they craved so desperately meant that Schweitzer would have to study medicine and thus abandon the career upon which he was already so well embarked. It meant giving up the books and studies he loved so much; it meant a surrender of the companionship of scholars, so dear to every intellectual, for the association with the most untutored of men.

The Challenge Accepted

It was a challenge to Schweitzer's courage and magnanimity. He accepted the challenge and cast his lot with the natives of the French Congo. He spent five years in the study of medicine, specializing in equatorial diseases that he might do his job well.

"I prepared," wrote Schweitzer, "to make three sacrifices: to abandon the organ, to renounce academic teaching activities . . . and to lose my financial independence . . . Now there happened to me what happened to Abraham, when he prepared to sacrifice his son. I, like him, was spared the sacrifice. The piano with pedal attachment built for the tropics . . . and the triumph of my own health over the tropical climate, allowed me to keep my skill on the organ.

"During the many quiet hours I was able to spend with Bach in the loneliness of the jungle, I penetrated more deeply into the spirit of his works. For the renunciation of my teaching activities at Strassburg University, I found compensation in opportunities for lecturing in others. If I did for a time lose my financial independence, I was able to win it again by means of organ and pen.

"That I was let off the threefold sacrifice I had already offered was for me the encouraging experience which in all the difficulties brought upon me . . . by the fateful post-war period has buoyed me up, and made me ready for every effort and every renunciation."

With his own hands Schweitzer built much of the hospital. For eight and even ten hours a day he stands at the operating table, bringing to these disease-ridden and poverty-stricken natives the relief they so desperately craved. Short of nurses, Schweitzer assists at this. His working day sometimes runs to eighteen hours.

"Only Through Love . . ."

Many of the natives of the Lambarene district are cannibals. When in search of human prey, they don the skins and claws of tigers and emit their howls. They think that in this manner they attain the ferocity of the animals. Sometimes at night Schweitzer is awakened by these tiger-like cries and has to hurry out to protect patients, recovering from operations, from the attacks of these cannibals.

At long intervals, he returns to raise funds by his concerts in the capitals of Europe for his hospital. Despite all his tasks, he finds time in the quiet hours of the night to write books on philosophy and science, which secure the attention of scholars as well as of the general public. Honors have come to him from many universities and from many countries.

In 1930, the city of Frankfurt conferred upon him the Goethe prize. In his address of acceptance, Schweitzer expressed his conviction of the essential sanctity of the human personality, regardless of race or color or conditions of life. "If that ideal is abandoned," he said, "the intellectual man goes to pieces and that means the end of culture and even of humanity."

The other great conviction which has been the guiding principle of his life is a profound belief in the supremacy of Christ's commandment of love. "The essential element in Christianity," says Schweitzer, "as it was preached by Jesus . . . is this, that it is only through love that we can attain to communion with God."

One of the most versatile men of our day is laboring at his little hospital in the African jungle, offering his rich talents and his consecrated spirit as a token of reparation for all the indignities, disease and sins which the white race has inflicted upon our black brothers. The scales may not yet balance, but Schweitzer has blazed a trail and set an example which, if followed often enough, may yet serve to make the reparation adequate. Among all the inhabitants of Africa, I wonder if there is a more courageous man than the Biblical scholar, theologian, philosopher, linguist, musician and surgeon who is wearing his life out in unwearying service to the most benighted and helpless of God's children.

Seldom does the white man hear him play any more upon the keyboard of Europe's great organ, but, there in the French Congo, Albert Schweitzer is playing upon the ebony keyboard of the Lambarenes a melody which stirs the hearts of men throughout the world. It is not the refrain of Bach which reaches us now. It is the melody of Christ's law of universal love put into glorious execution. When Schweitzer made his choice to abandon the lecture halls of Europe for the jungle of the Lambarenes, there were not wanting intellectuals who said his deed displayed the "courage of a fool." Yes, they are right. He is a fool: a fool for Christ.

Florence Nightingale

The name which has become a synonym for the highest ideals of the nursing profession is that of Florence Nightingale. To her vision, ability and courage are credited those sweeping reforms in the methods of caring for the sick which laid the foundations for the science of nursing. Though her social position necessitated her presentation at court, she had the courage to break with the traditions which doomed maidens of high-placed families to lives of social uselessness. Instead of frittering her time away with the inanities of court life, she devoted her time to studying the methods employed in hospitals, reformatories, and the other charitable institutions.

Around the middle of the last century, England was

sadly behind the times in matters of sanitation and nursing. Accordingly, Miss Nightingale made a tour of inspection of foreign hospitals. She had determined to make the alleviation of suffering her life work and she wished to neglect nothing that would make her proficient. After completing the course in nursing at Kaiserwerth, she went to Paris; here she studied the system of nursing and management in the hospitals under the charge of the Sisters of St. Vincent de Paul.

Her debt to the sisters was great indeed. Their painstaking care, their scrupulous cleanliness, their unwavering cheerfulness to their patients, as well as their gentleness, made a lasting impression upon the English girl. These she determined to incorporate into the system of nursing which she was to establish at home. This she did at the Governesses' Sanatorium in Harley Street.

A Trumpet Call

In 1854, England was stirred to its depths by the news of the sufferings of the sick and wounded in the Crimea. Great preparations had been made to equip the British soldiers with cannon, rifles, and supplies, but little thought had been given to caring for the wounded. The commonest preparations to carry out the first and simplest demands for the sick and injured of a large army were lacking. The insanitary conditions in the large barrack-hospital at Scutari were appalling. To Miss Nightingale this pressing human need sounded the trumpet call of duty.

She wrote immediately to Sidney Herbert, secretary of

war, offering her services. Her letter crossed with one from him inviting her to come to the Crimea.

On October 24th, she set out with a staff of thirty-seven nurses, partly volunteers, partly professionals trained in hospitals. On November 4th they reached Scutari, just in time to receive the Balaklava wounded. Miss Nightingale threw herself heart and soul into the work of easing the sufferings of these sick and wounded men. To see that these sufferers were properly ministered to, Miss Nightingale worked twenty hours at a stretch. She regularly took her place in the operating room and sought by her sympathy and tenderness to ease the pains of the sufferer. At night she would make her solitary round of the wards, stopping to speak a word of cheer at the bedside of each patient.

Soon, she had 10,000 men under her charge, and the general superintendence of all the hospitals on the Bosphorus. The death rate among the wounded in February, 1855, was as high as forty-two per cent. After a few months, however, when Miss Nightingale had effected numerous reforms in methods of sanitation and care, the rate sank as low as two per cent. Though stricken with fever, Miss Nightingale stuck to her post of duty till the work was done.

"Angle of Mercy"

The report of her labors stirred great enthusiasm in England, where she became known as the angel of mercy. A man-of-war was ordered to bring her home. London prepared to welcome her with national acclaim. With characteristic modesty, however, she returned quietly on a French ship, crossed to England, and escaped to her country home before the news of her return could leak out. "Perfect courage," says La Rochefoucauld, "is to do unwitnessed what we should be capable of doing before all the world." Miss Nightingale's valor did not spring from a multitude of witnesses, and she wanted no acclaim save the accolade of an approving conscience. Therein she found the source of both her courage and her strength.

Though her health was permanently impaired by her long ordeal in the Crimea, she devoted herself with calm courage to a life of quiet usefullness. With the £50,000 raised by a grateful nation in recognition of her services, she founded the Nightingale Home for training nurses at St. Thomas' and King's College Hospitals. She effected reforms in army sanitation and in army hospitals.

Her book, *Notes on Nursing,* gave an enormous stimulus to the development of the nursing profession. She helped in 1892 to organize a health crusade in Buckinghamshire. Teachers were sent out among the cottagers to give practical advice on such matters as drainage, ventilation, disinfectants, and cleanliness. If this plan were universally adopted, it would bring valuable knowledge to every home in England.

In 1907, King Edward VII insisted on conferring upon her the Order of Merit. At the venerable age of 90, full of years and of honor, she passed on. Her memory remains, however, as part of the noble heritage of the English people and an inspiration to mankind. Hers was a life of quiet courage. The turning point, it seems to me, occurred when she displayed the courage to break with the conventions which would have consigned her to the life of a social butterfly and cast her lot with the sick and wounded. They became her life-long clients. For them she became an adventurer, blazing new trails in the field of human service for the noblest of womanhood to follow.

Mahatma Gandhi

Out of the East have come from time immemorial great prophets, seers and mystics. But not for centuries did there come out of the Orient an ethical character of more impressive stature than Mahatma Gandhi. He towered above the statesmen and rulers of the world in utter simplicity of life, in asceticism, and in a sheer willingness to follow his conception of ethical principle at whatever cost to his political cause and to himself.

I know of no man who surpassed him in sheer moral courage. Even his enemies acknowledged the power of his indomitable will and his inexhaustible courage—a courage that led him into repeated, self-imposed fasts wherein he went about as close to death as man can go without entering that silent portal. A little man of skin and bones, weighing scarcely ninety pounds, wearing only a cloth from waist to knees, Gandhi pitted himself against the power of the mighty British Empire on many an occasion. Without arms or an army, relying only on the invincible might of moral power and the claims of the human soul to freedom, the Mahatma hurled defiance into the face of King and Parliament.

"Strike the chains of slavery from my people," he said, "and we shall cooperate. But on no other condition." His weapon was not violence but passive resistance, which he called soul force. More than any leader in the modern world, Gandhi infused ethical principles into political action and made them the lodestar of his policy.

"The idea-tight division of human activity into religious, social, and political compartments," Gandhi said, "is the prime fallacy of the modern world. If religion is not needed in politics, where on earth is it needed?"

He is a splendid illustration of the "terrible meek" who pit their gentleness, implemented only by the power of the moral law, against empires with tanks, battleships and bombing planes. He won the unquestioning loyalty of the vast millions of the Indian people because of the transparent unselfishness of his aims and the exalted holiness of his personal life. And he gave to the modern world a striking demonstration of the power of personal sanctity lit up by high intelligence.

"Get Out of Here"

Gandhi was not always so courageous. A study of his life discloses that, as a boy, he was timid and shy, and suffered from an inferiority complex. His conquest of fear, however, would seem to be as complete as any person in our generation has achieved. "The lad who dared not speak to anybody," observes Upton Close, "became the most fearless orator in India. The boy who was deathly afraid lest someone should poke fun at him, grew up to flount all accepted theories and manners of life, to dress only in a loin cloth, and to face trial and punishment as a felon, for the sake of his convictions." *

After completing his law course in England in 1891, Gandhi was sent by an Indian client to conduct a case in Pretoria, South Africa. The young lawyer set out on his mission with high hopes, little realizing the humiliations and the sufferings that were in store for him. Landing in South Africa, he found himself thrown off trains on which he had paid his fare, refused admission to hotels, and insulted on the streets.

One day, while walking in a park, he wandered innocently into a section where only the ruling race were permitted. A man on horseback struck him in the face with his whip. "Get out of here, you black ——," he swore, "and stay where you belong."

Discrimination, jeers, insults were his daily lot. The only members of the ruling race who showed some feeling for his people were the Christian missionaries. Their kindly interest prompted him to read that year some eighty books on Christianity. Thus was engendered in him a deep reverence for the teachings and the character of Jesus, which remained among the potent influences of his life.

Finding His Client

The injustice of the treatment meted out to him and to his people in South Africa kindled a slow flame of indignation within him. The leaders of the Indian community in Durban besought him to undertake a legal attack upon the legislation which discriminated against his countrymen.

---

* *The Living Age,* June, 1929, p. 278.

His people were helpless. Their only hope lay in this young barrister, skilled in the white man's law. Gandhi accepted the invitation. Then began the work that was destined to become the life work of Gandhi—the slow, painful process of wresting what measure of reluctant justice he could from the mass of discriminatory statutes which weighed like millstones around the necks of the Indian people.

The leaders of the Indian community were willing and able to pay him well. Gandhi, however, refused all fees. Instead of remaining for the one year in South Africa, as he had planned, Gandhi found it necessary to remain for twenty-three.

It was here that he founded in 1904 his first *ashram,* or retreat, in the form of an agricultural colony, fourteen miles from Durban, Natal. To that cooperative enterprise he turned over all his wealth, keeping for himself but two loin cloths. He was bidding a long farewell to the pride of life and to the things upon which the world sets so much store. No more was he to be known as the carefully groomed dandy, the clever lawyer, or even as a mere statesman. His people were soon to reverence him as the Great Soul, the Mahatma.

Returning to India in the summer of 1914, the Mahatma encouraged his people to support the British in the war on the strength of promises that long-sought reforms and liberties would be granted them. The war was won, but the Indians waited in vain for the promised freedom. The welled-up anger of his people was about to burst forth in destructive violence when Gandhi directed it into passive resistance. This involved mass civil disobedience to British law and proved a weapon of surprising effectiveness.

It required enormous discipline on the part of the masses to keep within the domain of non-violence, and into this work of training the Mahatma threw himself heart and soul. "It is an expression not of physical power," said Gandhi, "but of moral power. Right is its own defense." It welded the Indian people together as never before; it brought unity out of the heterogeneous masses of a disunited nation.

"Our Only Assurance"

In May 1921, there was a strike of 12,000 coolies in the tea gardens of Assam. This was followed by a railroad strike in Bengal with ensuing riots. A bloody outbreak of the fanatical Mohammedan Moplahs took place in Malabar in August. The situation was ripe for revolution to sweep the country like a prairie fire; the native troops, especially the Sikhs, awaited but a nod from Gandhi to rebel. The Mahatma, however, scorned the tempting voices of opportunism and expediency and stuck to his principles.

"The British," he said, "want us to put the struggle on the plane of machine guns. They have the weapons, and we have not. Our only assurance of beating them is to keep it on the plane where we have the weapons and they have not." That was on the moral plane.

It was on that plane that Gandhi issued his "declaration of war" to the Viceroy. In it he gave Lord Reading seven days to change the government's policy.

Here is a striking demonstration of the moral power that comes from the consciousness of the righteousness of a cause. Here, too, is the evidence of a conviction that, if a campaign is waged on a moral plane and, instead of being detoured or by-passed by irrelevant episodes of blind violence, is addressed to the conscience of a government, the largest measure of justice and right will result. This is based on the further conviction that all men have a moral nature which cannot remain permanently deaf to appeals persistently addressed to that tribunal enthroned by God in the soul of man.

Whether one accept his line of reasoning or not, there can be no denial that Gandhi forged a weapon of enormous power in his system of passive resistance, a weapon whose usefulness might well be explored in greater degree by other countries. True, rulers have traditionally shown impatience and even disdain for the slow weapons of the moral order to secure their ends and satisfy their imperious demands. It seems so much easier and quicker to smash their way through to their objectives by unleashing their instruments of slaughter and destruction.

If, however, the men whose tongues have been stilled by the millions could speak, would they not, we wonder, clamor with unyielding insistence upon all the governments of the world to work out their claims exclusively before the court of the moral order implemented with international sanctions. This may appear as something of a digression. It seems to me, however, to be the logical conclusion from Gandhi's premise—the insistence on keeping the contest on the moral plane.

Life of Self-Discipline

I spent a day with one of the disciples who lived with the Mahatma at his *ashram* or collective retreat; from this young Indian scholar I got an intimate glimpse of Gandhi's home life. When out of prison, he spent most of the year at his *ashram* at Segaon, near Wardha, one of the most primitive villages in India and inhabited largely by Untouchables. The members of his household could have no personal belongings, and were expected to do a certain amount of hand spinning every day. They arose before dawn, and divided most of the day between prayer and work.

The schedule which Gandhi himself followed was even more rigorous. For at least three decades he was a celibate as well as a vegetarian; the Gandhis had, however, four sons and several grandchildren. To help break down the barrier which for so long put the lowest caste beyond the pale of normal human life and intercourse, they adopted a girl from the Untouchables as their daughter. Here is moral courage in a superb degree.

Though thin almost as a skeleton, with wrinkled skin, bald head and a toothless smile, such charm and grace emanated from him that his enemies, British and Indian alike, sought to avoid personal encounters, lest they be made captive.

In March 1942, Britain's domination of India was threatened by the Japanese. Churchill had previously justified

British policy by saying, "two out of ten Englishmen depend on India." The threat of Japanese invasion, however, induced him to send Sir Stafford Cripps to beg the help of India, with the promise of Dominion Status after the war. Gandhi and his colleagues, remembering the glowing promises made during World War I and the oblivion in which they were largely buried after the war, countered with demands for freedom now. "We have no army," said Gandhi, "no military resources, no military skill, and non-violence is the only thing we can rely on—remember, I am more interested than the British in keeping the Japs out."

"The Best Bargain"

On August 8, speaking before Congress at the session which authorized a mass campaign of civil disobediance, Gandhi declared: "I do not want to be the instrument of Russia's defeat, nor China's. If that happens, I would hate myself." He nevertheless predicted a repetition of the disasters of Malaya, Singapore, and Burma, "unless Britain trusts the people of India to use their liberty in favor of the Allied cause." He promised furthermore: "If India is free, effective resistance could be offered against the aggressor."

The following day he was arrested and imprisoned in Aga Khan's palace near Poona. While there, in protest against the British policy of refusing freedom to his people, he underwent a fast of three weeks, which brought him deeper than ever into the valley of the shadow of death. "I always get the best bargains," he said, "from behind prison bars."

An analysis of Gandhi's work discloses the interesting and curious fact that though still a Hindu, he adopted the precepts of the Sermon on the Mount and endeavored to apply them with a definiteness and a literalness rarely found in the governments of so-called Christian countries. Many, if not most, of his ideals he drew from the winsome figure of Jesus. He inspired India with his own life of sacrifice and taught her moral principles to which political statesmen pay lip service but at which they often wink in practice.

Gandhi's greatness rested primarily in his exalted moral character; secondly, in his political leadership of his people. His methods have led to the achievement of complete liberty and independence, and he will go down as the creator of the Indian nation that has now emerged. History will acclaim him as the Father of India; that is no small title to enduring fame.

"Reactionary or revolutionary," says Nehru, his friend and disciple, "Gandhi has changed the face of India, given pride and character to a cringing and demoralized people, built up strength and consciousness in the masses, and made the Indian problem a world problem."

Possessing neither guns, nor tanks, nor bombing planes, and relying only on the invincible power of the naked human soul conscious of the righteousness of its cause, Gandhi restored a sense of racial dignity to the Indian people, beaten down by the rifle butts of the West.

Pale, ascetic, fasting often, spending long hours in communion with God, from whom he derived his strength and his courage, Mahatma Karamchand Gandhi towered above the statesmen of the world in his noble scorn of physical force and in his determination to keep the controversies with the oppressors of his nation upon the moral plane. That is the only plane upon which disputes between rational creatures should ever be put, for it is only before the court of reason and conscience that the problems of justice and right agitating mankind can ever be properly settled. Assassinated while on his way to lead his people in prayer Gandhi has gone down in history occupying a unique niche—that of a saint among the statesmen of the world.

Father Damien

The last instance I shall cite of courage among the adventurers for mankind is that of Father Damien, Martyr of Molokai. His story can be told briefly and simply. It is, however, full of eloquence and of inspiration. It is a story of a quiet, serene courage that stays with the ship till the last deed of human service has been rendered, and then goes down into the fathomless waters. It is the story of a courage that seeks out the most miserable of God's children on the loneliest outpost, and ministers to them with mind and heart and soul until death writes *finis* to the labors. For more than thirty years the saga of Father Damien's labors at Molokai has played a melody on the keys of my memory, a melody whose undertones whispered of service to mankind and whose overtones spoke of consecration to God.

Biding farewell to the pleasures and gaieties of the world, a Belgian boy, Joseph de Veuster, offered himself to the Society of the Sacred Hearts of Jesus and Mary to go as a missionary to the islands in the South Pacific. Not only did he renounce all property, but he stripped himself even of his very name, taking simply the name of Damien.

Ordained in Honolulu on May 24, 1864, Father Damien ministered to the natives of Hawaii. At that time it was the practice of the Hawaiian government to deport its lepers to the island of Molokai. The lot of these unfortunate victims was pitiable indeed. The government was unable to provide them with either resident physicians or nurses.

As long as the lepers were able to care for themselves, they were not so badly off. "But as soon as the dreadful disease renders them helpless," wrote the Superintendent of Health, "it would seem that even demons themselves would pity their condition and hasten their relief." Without physicians, nurses or priest—and many of the 600 lepers so badly eaten by the disease that they could not dress even their own sores—they were a pathetic spectacle. It was to this colony of outcasts, shunned even by the Molokaian natives as "unclean," that Father Damien asked to be sent as their resident pastor.

A Triple Role

Bishop Maigret acceded. On May 10, 1873, Father Damien arrived at the colony where he was to labor the rest of his life. For a long time Father Damien played, as best he could, the triple role of priest, physician and nurse. With his own hands he dressed their ulcers, washed their feverish faces, built little homes for them, made coffins and even dug their graves. He was the minister general to all their varied needs.

When melancholy was biting into them and black despair was knocking at their hearts, Father Damien bent low over their bedside and whispered words of spiritual comfort. He reminded them of the promise made by Christ in the Sermon on the Mount: "Blessed are they that mourn; for they shall be comforted." He spoke to them not only in words but in the more persuasive language of deeds. The force of his own example, the daily sacrifice of himself for his flock, let something of the spirit of God shine through the stained glass of his own personality. Like him, they sought to sublimate their sufferings and turn their adversity to spiritual gain.

Father Damien championed the cause of the lepers before the Hawaiian government. His appeals resulted in improvements in the water supply, the dwellings and the victualling of the settlement. The asceptic precautions current today were lacking then. After twelve years of unremitting ministry, including the frequent dressing of their sores, Father Damien contracted the disease; this, he knew, had been only a matter of time. Undaunted, he continued bravely at this work until four years later. On April 15, 1889, the dread disease stilling his gallant heart, and making idle his busy hands, released him from his self-imposed prison house.

His deathbed scene I shall never forget. It was portrayed with vivid realism at the International Missionary Exposition in Rome in 1925. Father Damien is lying propped up in bed; his face is swollen and distorted; ulcers make it hard to look at. One tends to turn away from the gruesome sight. Kneeling about his bedside, however, are those who do not turn away—the abandoned lepers for whom he has given his life. Within that mass of festering flesh they know there is the soul of one of God's noblemen. Their lips are moving in prayer; there is a tear in their wistful eyes and their hearts are heavy; for they know that they are losing the best friend that God has ever given to them in this world.

Index of Courage

An index of courage is the willingness to make sacrifices. Joseph de Veuster had given up just about everything dear to the human heart. He had given up his beloved Belgium, never to see it again. He had given up his own name, dearer to most people than their pocket books, hiding himself from the praises of men under the name of a saint. He had left father and mother, sister and brother, kinsfolk, the possibility of wife and children, that he might become all things to the most neglected of God's children —the lepers of Molokai. Here was a courage that gave all. "Courage," observes C. C. Colton, "is generosity of the highest order, for the brave are prodigal of the most precious things."

The name of Father Damien, Martyr of Molokai, hangs over the island like a benediction from on high. On the scroll of the world's heroes, his name stands as a symbol of courage and sacrifice. Father Damien had become an adventurer for mankind, a blazer of new trails in social altruism, a fool for God.

In answer to every great human need arises a great courage. Among the starving poor of Paris, Frederick Ozanam found his client and his courage. In the slums of Osobe, Kagawa heard his call. In the crouching figure of a Negro slave in the Colmar market place, Schweitzer found a challenge that would not let him go. In the cries of the sick and wounded in the Crimea, without elementary nursing care, Florence Nightingale heard the trumpet call to duty. In the downtrodden Indians of South Africa, discriminated against at every turn, Gandhi found his true vocation. In the festering lepers at Molokai, abandoned to their forlorn fate by their own people, Father Damien discovered his life-long apostolate.

An Unfailing Source

From the espousal of these great human needs was born the courage to implement their high commitments. Here is an unfailing source of courage—the dedication of oneself to a cause that transcends not only one's selfish interests but one's very life as well. Out of the clear perception of the surpassing value of a noble undertaking is begotten the willingness to risk life and limb, and that which costs as much—a life of rebuffs, unwearying labor and sacrifice. That, after all, is the meaning of courage. It is the story, ancient yet ever new, of losing one's life for a noble cause only to find it.

It is the story of all the saints and heroes and martyrs of the race. They gave up all only to have all and more flung back to them. They are the dreamers of dreams and the movers of the world. Truly can they say:

World losers and world forsakers,
Upon whom the pale man beams,
Yet we are the movers and shakers
Of the world forever, it seems.

There is a connection then between courage, especially of the moral type, and vision. "The charm of the best courages," observes Emerson, "is that they are inventions, inspirations, flashes of genius." Courage implies an ear sensitive to the cry of human needs, and a heart generous enough to respond, no matter what the cost. From these visions and high commitments spring the enthusiasms and the inspirations which lift life from the foothills to the peaks of true nobility. "The best of life," says H. J. Desmond, "are its 'white moments,' its ardors and enthusiasms, its irradiations and its consecrations, which though they stay with us but a minute, carry us farther along toward the goal than all our toil and moil."

If these great moments with their beckonings to the surrender of self for the consecrated service of human need in all its myriad forms are neglected, our lives henceforth are set in shallows and in miseries. "The golden moments in the stream of life," observes George Eliot, "rush past us, and we see nothing but sand; the angels come to visit us, and we only know them when they are gone." Alas and alack! for those who let these great moments with their challenges go unanswered. Ozanam, Kagawa, Schweitzer, Nightingale, Gandhi, Father Damien were keen-eyed and big-hearted enough to seize these white moments of challenge and of inspiration, these radiant beams from God, and erect them into lives of towering service for human need. They shoved forward the frontiers of social altruism, become adventurers for mankind, fools for God.

Summary

An individual must view himself not only as a citizen of a particular country but also as a citizen of the world. He must learn to say with ever increasing awareness: "My country is the world. My countrymen are all mankind." To act upon this principle requires a kind of moral courage which has been all too rare, but which is desperately needed to heal a wounded and ailing world today. The key to the development of this form of moral courage, humanitarian and world-wide in scope, lies in the clear realization of two fundamental truths:

(1) The personality of each individual, regardless of race or creed, possesses a dignity and a sanctity that stems from the fact that it is an image of god.

(2) Whatever we do to a human being is to be regarded as being done to God himself.

By focusing our attention upon these two basic truths, we make them psychologically strong and render them functional ideals in motivating our conduct so that we have the courage to be fools for God and servants to all mankind.

RULE 7. *Throw yourself into the task of fighting for the underdog, helping the underprivileged, lifting up the downtrodden, bringing comfort to the suffering and promoting the happiness of others, in all of whom you can see the lineaments of the face of Christ, who will reward you for such actions as bountifully as if they were done to Him; thus do you develop the courage, to be servants of mankind and fools for God.*

Reflect upon the instances of courage cited in this chapter and wait until tomorrow to read the next chapter.

Chapter Eight

THE STAIRS OF ADVERSITY

There is some soul of goodness in things evil,
Would men observingly distil it.
—Shakespeare, *Henry V,* IV, 1

When adversity overtakes *an individual, there is a tendency to react emotionally, to bemoan one's ill fortune and to give way to self-pity. He becomes petulant, gloomy and despondent. While in this mood, anxiety takes root and brings forth her brood of haunting fears, pervading every item of his thought and crippling his every act. Drifting through his personality like an invisible mist of chlorine gas, anxiety poisons the wellsprings of joy and clouds his sleep with suffocating dread.*

How can one develop courage in the presence of adversity and affliction? "Forget about the disturbing situation," is the advice commonly given. "Think of something else. Take in a movie. Get a couple drinks. Do anything, so long as it takes your mind off the matter."

Psychiatry orders the direct opposite. Face the situation, frankly, calmly, realistically. If you run away from the disturbing matter, it pursues you and quickly overtakes you. Try to ignore it, and the focus of infection widens. The anxiety shoots over into other phases of your conscious life. Soon, complexes are formed and you are a psychic cripple.

The ostrich policy of burying one's head in the sand to escape unpleasant realities is foolish and ineffective. It reaches the maximum of folly in dealing with adversity, afflictions, handicaps. A wound that is ignored and exposed to every contamination will not long escape infection. The poison will spread throughout the whole system; so it is with a psychic wound inflicted by the obsessing anxiety springing from some affliction or adversity.

The cure consists in bathing the wound with the antiseptic of sustained attention. Look the adversity in the eye; analyze the affliction and see how it can be overcome or at least be borne with patience until time and resourcefulness have transmuted the liability into an asset. The more severe the crisis, the greater is the need for prolonged thought and calm analysis. Instead of allowing the steam-roller of fate to crush him flat, the calm thoughtful persons climbs upon it and uses it to crush the obstacles in his path.

Of all the activities in which man engages, thinking is the most rewarding. It bestows its richest dividends when the going gets tough and the road ahead is obscured. "To rectify the distortions which create fear," points out Dr. T. A. Williams, "straightforward introspection is absolutely essential." Out of such careful analysis of the adversity will come a way of dealing with it, not emotionally but realistically. What matters most in life is not what befalls us, but how we react to such incidents.

With clarity of vision and adherence to high ideals it is

always possible for the courageous soul to distil goodness out of an evil brew, to transform obstacles into stepping stones and to rise on the ladder of handicaps. On the principle that an ounce of illustration is worth a ton of theory, we shall cite a number of incidents showing you how individuals through facing adversity with clear vision, steadfast adherence to ideals and unwavering trust in God have secured the courage to transform adversity into a stairs on which they have scaled the heights.

Authentic Expression

Courage finds its most authentic expression in the face of adversity and in the shadow of defeat. Hardship, handicap, suffering constitute the testing grounds of the iron virtue. It is easy to maintain one's poise when the going is smooth and easy. To preserve one's serenity, however, when the going gets tough, and the storm of adversity tosses one's bark at menacing angles on the high seas, is immensely more difficult.

For this achievement courage is required. Indeed, one of the most important uses of this noble virtue is to capitalize adversity, to rise on the ladder of handicaps, to transform obstacles into stepping stones and to turn defeat into victory. Courage is thus seen to be the spiritual counterpart of the magic alchemy for which the ancients sought in their efforts to transmute the baser metals into gold.

As there are few elements in life more certain than hardships and adversities, it is important for one to learn as early as possible how to face them with fortitude and valor. To endure them with what resignation one can command is one thing; to use them for one's spiritual growth and improvement of character is vastly more important.

Unless the effort is intelligently made to adjust our sails to utilize a cross wind, our bark will be tossed hither and thither, the mere plaything of every wind that blows. The wise captain, however, will not allow his bark to be driven out of its course by unfriendly winds but will adjust his sails to bend the power of the elements to assist him in reaching his own goal. Here is the pattern for all of us to follow in the spiritual sphere.

It is in accordance with the manner in which we face the problems of adversity that the streams of character flow to far-dissevered destinies. The individual who reacts to an unexpected handicap, to a stinging defeat, by cries of petulance and complaint, not only extracts no good from his ordeal but allows it to coarsen his character. He becomes sour, morose, vindictive; life becomes for him a game of blindman's buff, without meaning or purpose. That there are legions who react in this futilitarian way the literature of our day gives evidence. People are dismayed by the catastrophe of global war; they are appalled by the prospect of famine and chaos following in its wake.

"Something in Ourselves"

True, it is a time to try men's souls. Never will dawn the day, however, when catastrophes and disasters will not afflict us. The center of man's equilibrium must be within him; otherwise, he will be as unstable as a weathervane. It is not so much what befalls one, as how he *reacts* to the vicissitude, that really matters. The crucial factor, the stabilizer, the alchemizer, lies within. Before the dawn of the Christian era the Stoic philosopher, Epictetus, caught a glimmering of this truth, when he said: "The condition and characteristic of a philosopher is that he expects all hurt and benefit from himself."

When we look deeply into ourselves, we find that we are what we are, not so much because of what things and people have done to us, but because of the manner in which we have habitually responded to those occurrences. The volitional element within ourselves is the decisive factor. Cassius reflects the conviction of thinkers, both ancient and modern, when he declares:

The fault, dear Brutus, is not in the stars,
But in ourselves, that we are underlings.

This is the point of a modern play, *Dear Brutus,* in which the author, Sir James Matthew Barrie, whimsically develops the thought stated in these two lines of Shakespeare. It is not fate or accident which forces us to do things, he has one character clearly say, but "something in ourselves," that allows us to go on acting in the same foolish way over and over again.

Whether we do the fool thing or the wise thing, it is the *element within* which so directs. We are not the flotsam and jetsam of cosmic tides; we are the products of our own sculpturing.

A study of the biography of men and women who have left their footprints on the sands of time shows that the decisive factor in their achievements was not external, but internal. Indeed, some of the characters whose accomplishments provoke the abiding admiration of mankind reached their eminence by climbing the ladder of adversity and by converting obstacles into stepping stones.

The Ladder of Handicaps

The most impressive name in all medicine is that of Louis Pasteur. Because of the titanic work he accomplished we are likely to imagine him a man of robust health. The fact is, however, that at forty-six he suffered a paralytic stroke which handicapped him the rest of his life. The work of Charles Darwin in biology is indeed prodigious, yet he was dogged by continuous illness, scarcely knowing a day of perfect health.

Robert Louis Stevenson suffered from tuberculosis from which he could find no escape, yet, with this affliction eating into his lungs, he achieved one of the high places in English literature. Milton was blind, but he wrote poetry with a majesty of diction that has rarely been surpassed. He illustrates the truth of Emerson's observation: "Whilst man sits on the cushion of advantages, he goes to sleep. When he is pushed, tormented, defeated, he has a chance to learn something; he has been put on his wits, on his manhood; he has gained facts; learns his ignorance; is cured of the insanity of conceit; has got moderation and real skill."

Beethoven was deaf. He wrote his great symphonies, however, in spite of that crippling affliction—symphonies he was to hear only in his inner ear. Demosthenes had a weak voice and he stammered. Instead of allowing these deficiencies to frustrate him in his ambition, he made them serve as stimulants to indefatigable zeal. Declaiming against the noise of waves, and with pebbles in his mouth, he achieved first rank among the orators of the world. Helen Keller was blind and deaf; in spite of this double obstacle, she managed to achieve a high education and to write with distinction about the culture of the race.

Bedridden for twenty-five years, Stanton Kirkham undertook to capitalize his long illness by writing a book of absorbing interest, *Shut-In.* "As the most barren regions of the earth," he writes, "yield something to the botanist and the geologist, the most desolate aspects of life are not wholly without interest to the philosopher." Here is the determination to make his very affliction yield its measure of fruit.

Expressing the determination of all these handicapped people, Beethoven cried out: "If I were only rid of this affliction I could embrace the world! . . . No! I cannot endure it! *I will seize fate by the throat;* most assuredly it shall not get me wholly down." Tortured by their affliction, they did not lie down before it; they seized it by the throat; they transformed it from an obstacle into a stepping stone.

"Courage Makes Them Favorable"

In the determination to face one's handicaps not petulantly, but realistically, constructively, changing them into the rungs of a ladder by which to reach one's purposed goal, courage plays a decisive role. The timid bleats out his sense of futility in useless sighs or in vain gnashing of teeth: the brave man buckles on his armor, mounts upon his affliction as upon a spirited steed, and rides to his rendezvous with high destiny.

In the analysis of all the noble souls who seized adversity by the throat, and compelled it to do their bidding, courage will be found to be in the driver's seat. "Who, then," observes Epictetus, "is the invincible man? He whom nothing that is outside the sphere of his moral purpose can dismay." Let adversities, hardships, handicaps, afflictions fall like thunder from the sky; the courageous soul marches on, undeterred, to his high goal.

Many timid souls are forever waiting for the dawning of the day when all the circumstances will be in just the right tune for the achievement of the long postponed project—writing the book, composing the symphony, painting the picture, building the bridge. Always, however, there is a discordant note, and the cherished project gradually fizzles out in the effervescence of merely good intentions which constitute the proverbial pavement of the netherworld. Men in whose souls the iron chord of courage is sounding, however, seize adversity by the throat and make the most unpropitious circumstances minister to the accomplishment of their objective.

While languishing in jail, Bunyan wrote *Pilgrim's Progress,* Cervantes composed *Don Quixote,* Sir Walter Raleigh his *History of the World.* Some of the best of O. Henry's stories were written in a jail cell, and some of the most radiant works of Toyohiko Kagawa were composed in the austere and forbidding quarters of a Japanese prison. Courage does not wait for circumstances to become favorable. It *makes* them favorable.

Under what adverse circumstances did Handel compose his *Messiah?* "His health and his fortunes," says a biographer, "had reached the lowest ebb. His right side had become paralyzed and his money was all gone; his creditors seized him and threatened him with imprisonment. For a brief time he was tempted to give up the fight—but then he rebounded again to compose the greatest of his inspirations, the epic *Messiah.*" Teetering on the thin edge of hopelessness, his courage returned and he transmuted these distressing circumstances into the provocatives of his mighty work, with its immortal "Hallelujah Chorus." Truly did Emerson remark: "What a new face courage puts on everything!"

Like a spark of electricity, courage galvanizes a moody and petulant individual into action, which is the best way to "snap out" of a spell of despondency.

Distilling Goodness out of Evil

Because of a hunting accident, Henry Fawcett lost his eyesight when he was only twenty-six, yet he determined to go on with his career. He became a professor of political economy at Cambridge University and subsequently a member of Parliament; he served as Postmaster-General of England from 1880 till his death in 1884. He has left a record of cheerfulness and courage that remains to this day. He was fond of repeating the lines of Henry V at the battle of Agincourt:

There is some soul of goodness in things evil,
Would men observingly distil it.

Sorrow, grief, shame, humiliation can easily lead to brooding, melancholy and despair. It requires courage to check and discipline them and make them yield their proper fruit. That fruit is tenderness, sympathy, kindliness, amendment. Only those who have themselves suffered sorrow and humiliation can really understand the lot of those bowed down by these heavy burdens. The shining Apollo, drinking in the paeans of praise in the hour of victory, may be the envy of many. He is but an infant, however, in the realm of sympathy and understanding when compared with those whose hearts have been rent by a great sorrow or crushed by a devastating shame.

Out of those wounded hearts comes a tenderness that fain would spare others the pains which they have borne. "I know what suffering means," said a friend of mine who had endured bitter humiliation, "and I would not want to bring pain to a single living creature. I do not think," he added, "that I could ever henceforth step even upon a worm."

The noblest line in Thornton Wilder's play, *The Angel That Troubled the Waters,* expresses its central truth: "In Love's service only the wounded soldiers can serve." Why? Because only they know the meaning of pain. Only they have the delicate tenderness of touch which comes from such an experience. Only they who have suffered know the meaning of love.

The Key to Understanding

Suffering and humiliation borne with courage engender sensitivity which is the key to sympathy and understanding.

It is the source both of our terror and of our glory. Out of Mozart's great suffering came his great symphonies. Out of the humiliations which bowed Francis Thompson's head in shame came the matchless poetry of *The Hound of Heaven.* Out of the excruiating torture of Calvary's Cross came the love which found expression in the words of forgiveness to the penitent thief: "This day thou shalt be with me in paradise." Out of every great affliction borne with courage comes the love which finds articulation in Elizabeth Barrett Browning's noble lines:

. . . The widest land
Doom takes to part us, leaves thy heart in mine
With pulses that beat double. What I do
And what I dream include thee, as the wine
Must taste of its own grapes. And when I sue
God for myself, He hears that name of thine,
And sees within my eyes, the tears of two.

Courage is able to tear from the black robe of sorrow its hidden silver lining. Courage is able to take the lashes of shame and use them for one's betterment. Courage is able to drain the chalice of suffering to its bitter dregs and transmute the pain not into resentment but into understanding, forgiveness, love. Courage can transform the wreath of thorns into a crown of joy; it can transmute the cross from a symbol of shame and ignominy into a banner of honor and glory.

If the person upon whom a crushing humiliation falls will have the courage to take it calmly and patiently, he can use it as a stepping stone to a life of greater virtue.

Let him look the humiliation courageously in the face and say: "Yes, I see now, bitter as is my shame, that this path leads the wrong way. I will make this serve as a flash of lightning illuminating the whole landscape of my journeying, and I will choose a better path." In this way he can make it serve his deepest needs instead of inflicting upon him merely blind suffering.

How many a man has been saved from ultimate ruin and disgrace by a hard jolt which he took in a realistic and brave manner! Pain is nature's warning. Only those who are valorous enough to face it honestly, however, read its meaning and profit by its warning. No sorrow need ever be suffered without being made to distil its measure of help and of ultimate joy. Against the background of shipwreck, imprisonment, fasting, labors, stripes, perils and suffering, St. Paul was able to say: "Rejoice in the Lord always: again I say, rejoice."

Without suffering, there is no sympathy; without hardship, there is no hardihood; without the cross, there is no crown. Back of every great virtue there has been the courageous bearing of a great cross. Sorrow bravely borne tells us in her silence more than pleasure with all her clamorous revelry. Robert Browning Hamilton thus contrasts these two attendants upon mankind:

I walked a mile with Pleasure,
She chattered all the way,
But left me none the wiser
For all she had to say.

I walked a mile with sorrow,
And ne'er a word said she;
But, oh, the things I learned from her
When Sorrow walked with me!

The President of the Newman Club at the University of Illinois and one of the most popular students on the campus a number of years ago was Frank Schrepfer. The load of handicaps he bore would have strangled the ambition of most young men, but not Frank. He came back from World War I minus his right arm, his body riddled with shrapnel, with one-sixth normal vision. Yet, with the aid of a reader, he achieved high grades, became probably the ablest orator on the campus, won his degree with distinction, and became an outstanding expert in landscape architecture.

Far from complaining about his handicaps, he was the soul of cheerfulness and infected with his good spirits all with whom he came in contact. He was a walking illustration of the power of courage to distil from misfortune a noble and inspiring character. "All sunshine," runs an Arab proverb, "makes Sahara." But storms and tempests fashion a picturesque landscape. "Live unto the dignity of thy nature," said Sir Thomas Browne, "and leave it not disputable at last whether thou hast been a man." Frank Schrepfer so capitalized his handicaps as to put the result beyond all dispute.

An Amazing Case

Edison Marshall tells the amazing story of a girl who

rose upon a handicap which would have imprisoned most people in an invalid's room for life. He was sailing from Seattle for Western Alaska. On the first night out he noticed a group of people watching a card game; to his amazement, he found that one of the players was a young girl who was using her feet to play.

A slim, pretty girl of about eighteen, she was leaning far back in her chair, holding her cards with one foot and playing them skillfully with the other. She had slashed off her stockings just above the instep so that the bared portions of her feet were about the size of hands. Why was she playing with her feet instead of with her hands? Was this a circus stunt? His question was answered when he perceived that under the girl's tight-drawn cape there were no arms.

Determined to get better acquainted with the vivacious girl, he invited her the following evening to dance. With a smile she rose to her feet, and coming close to him stepped off to the music. She was not a brilliant dancer, but not a dub at it either. Without arms, her balance was precarious, but she had persisted in the effort until she could dance passably well. Gradually, she unfolded the story of her long fight against her crippling handicap to live a normal life.

"When I first discovered that I was different from other children, my impulse was to hide," she said. "To be born misshapen was gruesome, an affront to humanity, I thought. It was not as though I had been born whole and lost my arms in an accident. The sight of people like me often causes other people to lose their appetites. For a while I wanted to die, but the thought came to me that perhaps I needn't sicken people. If I tried hard to appear and act normal, possibly I would seem nearly normal to others.

"The hardest part was to come out of hiding. That meant not only to associate with other children, but to be perfectly frank about not having any arms. If the other children wanted to see, I showed them. My face burned, but I showed them just the same. I never cried in public, no matter what happened; as often as I could, I would laugh. Perhaps you don't know that laughter is a habit, but I know that people can teach themselves to laugh if their lives depend upon it.

"I couldn't stand to be pitied, so I never stopped practicing. I think I practiced even in my sleep. And I did everything I could to make myself attractive. After a while—and I tell you it has saved my soul—I found that my very affliction could be made interesting instead of horrible. Instead of an affront to humanity, I could become in a way a compliment to it; I could show people what wonderful resources the body has."

"And what wonderful strength the human spirit has," Marshall said.*

She had compelled her handicap to minister to her attractiveness. A stimulating conversationalist, she dressed in the latest vogue, adroitly accentuating her best features and diverting the eye from her narrow shoulders.

The uses to which she put her feet seem incredible. Sitting in an officer's cabin, she reached for a fountain pen

* "Drama in Real Life," *Reader's Digest,* April 1943, p. 45.

in a wire rack, unscrewed its cap, wrote in a good "hand," and then casually replaced the pen. She knitted by the hour, displaying a mastery of the needle which many women never achieve. She powdered her nose, gestured, held a glass upon the sole of her foot with her agile toes, ate at the table with the rest of the passengers, turned the pages of books and newspapers and smoked a cigarette with ease and grace.

Feats which lay skeptics and even doctors would have argued were impossible because of the bone structure of the human body, this young lady did with ease. She had made of herself not only a normal but a radiant personality. She was a living demonstration of the power of courage to overcome an enormous handicap and to convert it into a stepping stone to inspiring achievement.

Few are the obstacles which can frustrate the naked human soul when endowed with moral courage. Over the frustration the soul climbs to sublimity. This young girl demonstrated that people, in whose souls the iron chord of courage is echoing, are in the words of Shakespeare

. . . not a pipe for fortune's finger
To sound what stop she please.

The Courage to Rise

Courage lies at the bottom of hope and of redemption. Few indeed are the people who go through life like a shining Apollo without ever stumbling along the way. Mistakes of mind and of heart spell out most of the history of the race. "Life," remarks a character in the play,

Madame X, "is just one mistake after another—all the way to the top!" It is human to err, and divine to forgive. The French have a proverb which says: "To understand all is to pardon all."

While mistakes, shortcomings, sins, are part of the experience of every human being, the courageous soul will not remain lying down, but will rise up every time he falls. His falls will become less frequent, and ultimately he will attain a high stability of noble conduct which is one of the most precious achievements of life. The man without courage who falls is likely to remain in that state. Dereliction follows upon the heels of dereliction, for the tides of psychological aspiration work against him.

Who is there who, having fallen, does not find it easier to indulge in a fresh lapse? What difference will another dereliction make, he asks, since I am already in moral exile? It is of supreme importance for an individual to combat this defeatist philosophy by lifting himself up at once, seeking in humility and penitence the pardon of the Most High, and rallying all his forces to prevent a relapse. Let him say with the prodigal son: "I will rise, and will go to my father, and say to him: Father, I have sinned against heaven, and before thee; I am not worthy to be called thy son; make me as one of thy hired servants."

The mercy he will receive from his Heavenly Father is mirrored in the Scriptural narrative. "And when he was a great way off, his father saw him, and was moved with compassion, and running to him, fell upon his neck, and kissed him. . . . And the father said to his servants: Bring forth quickly the first robe, and put it on him, and put a ring on his hand, and shoes on his feet: And bring hither the fatted calf, and kill it, and let us eat and make merry: Because this my son was dead, and is come to life again: was lost and is found." *

The makings of character include handicaps, deficiencies, troubles, even moral lapses. They are the raw material out of which strong and noble character can ultimately be fashioned through courage, penitence and the grace of God, which is never wanting to those who try.

"One must think of one's sins," observed a fearful and worried soul.

"So as to repent them, yes," replied the priest-novelist John Ayscough. "After that as little as possible."

"It is not so much things which bother a man," observed Montaigne, "as the opinion he has about things." We have it in our power to allow them to bother us or to dismiss them as unwelcome intruders. The decision rests with us.

"A Pure Cross"

"Annoyance with ourselves tends to dishearten us, to fill us with the sensitiveness of self-love, to discourage us in the service of God, to impede our progress, to make us seek relief in ways contrary to grace, to wither and distract us, to exhaust the soul and prepare the way for repugnance and despair of perseverance," says Fenelon in his *Spiritual Counsels.* "Nothing hinders our souls more than interior vexation with our faults when we yield to it voluntarily. But if we bear with ourselves and our imperfections, without consenting to the dictates of self-love, then

* *Luke,* 15:18f.

the suffering caused to us is a pure cross, and consequently a means of grace. Let such suffering pass by, as we would let an attack of fever or a headache pass, without doing anything that could aggravate the evil."

The harried soul who is forever mulling over past mistakes and derelictions worries himself sick and depletes the store of energy and hope. Let the sins of the past be repented. Then let them be buried in the graves of the past, without forever digging up the skeletons and dangling them as gruesome spectres before one's terrified gaze. It is necessary to live in the living present and to summon courage anew to face the tasks of each new day.

Worry not o'ermuch o'er future,
Nor regret the past too late.
They who struggle with the present
Move the hand that shapes our fate.

That great student of the spiritual life, Father Mateo Crawley-Boevey, tells of a scrupulous person who was forever returning to her spiritual father, confessing the same sin over and over again and with apparent concern that it had never been forgiven. Wishing to teach her a much needed lesson, the confessor asked:

"What other sin have you committed?"

"None," she replied.

"Oh, yes," he said. "You have failed to mention the greatest of all."

"What is that?" she asked in horror.

"You doubted the mercy of God. That is the *capital* sin."

"Go, Then, and Learn . . ."

In his masterpiece, *The Following of Christ,* Thomas a Kempis brings help and courage to all worried souls with the following counsel:

"Son, patience and humility under adversity please Me more than much consolation and devotion in prosperity. . .

"Man thou art, and not God; thou are flesh not an angel.

"How canst thou continue ever in the same state of virtue, when this was wanting to the angels in heaven, and to the first man in Paradise?

"I am He who raiseth up to safety them that mourn; and them that know their own infirmity I promote to My own divinity."

In those words of the holy writer one catches an echo of the voice of Christ saying: "Go then and learn what this meaneth: I will have mercy and not sacrifice." And of that other utterance of the Master to the crowd about to stone to death the woman taken in the sin of adultery: "He that is without sin among you, let him first cast a stone at her."

No more striking case of the courage to rise from a long career of sensual living to a life of virtue and nobility is afforded in all history than that of St. Augustine of Hippo. At seventeen he was the father of a son born out of wedlock; for fifteen years he was held in the thralldom of a paramour. Often did he cry: "Give me chastity." But then, fearful of the restraints that would entail, he would add: "But not yet." The *yet* was a long time coming—not for lack of light but for lack of a willingness to put his house in order. Finally, he arose from his bondage. With one of the most valorous thrusts in history, he cut the Gordian knot that bound him to a sensual past and plunged into a new life of virtue and holiness. Not only did he abandon the profligate ways of the past, but he applied himself with such zeal to works of penitence and virtue that the fragrance of his holiness spread far and wide.

His two great books, *Confessions* and *The City of God,* belong to general literature and appeal to every soul. The *Confessions,* in which he tells with humility and shame of his dalliance with sensual vice, mirrors a theology which has been fused in the crucible of a single life and narrates the history of God's actions upon the individual soul. *The City of God* is theology framed in the history of humanity and describes the action of God upon the world at large.

His resurrection from a career of sensuality to a life of heroic sanctity will long remain as a testimony of the power of a courageous soul to break the shackles of the past and embark upon a new path. It remains as a rainbow in the skies, giving light and hope and courage to all who are striving to achieve a similar resurrection.

Religion Inspires Courage

For the conquest of moral handicaps and the escape from the bondage of evil habits, religious faith is of first importance. One can consult a psychiatrist, unfold the past endlessly to a psychoanalyst, and visit the psychologist times without end, and still remain in the toils of sensual practice. Religion brings the sinner face to face with his God. The individual who turns to God in prayer never finds his prayer unanswered. No one can be long in the presence of a genuinely good person without being ashamed of his evil doing. No one can place himself repeatedly in the presence of God, the Source of all virtue and the Author of all holiness, without having his conscience quickened and his heart purified.

Like an opiate, sin drugs a conscience to drowsiness and stupor; prayer stabs it wide awake. One of the basic factors causing the disintegration of personality and filling the mind with phobias, complexes and mental tics is the sense of guilt. Such persons plague the psychiatrist for relief, when relief is within their reach. Turning to God in penitence and prayer will work wonders for the soul burdened and restless with its sense of guilt.

Religion constitutes a powerful ally of the individual who endeavors to face the trials and adversities of life with fortitude and courage. Why? Because it brings before his mind the Supreme Being who is alone the Guarantor of the rational organization of the universe and the Underwriter of its moral values. "There are no eternal values," observes Professor William Ernest Hocking, "unless there are eternal valuers." Life cannot be "a tale told by an idiot, full of sound and fury, signifying nothing." Why? Because God is infinite wisdom and the work of His hands cannot be without meaning or purpose.

Religion clothes all life, even the dreariest of our days and the most menial of our labors, with a transcendental value and a divine significance. Religion stands as a reminder of the infinite worth of the human soul and of the sanctity of the human personality. It therefore gives the assurance which every sojourner on this planet in the skies so sorely needs at times—that he *does* matter, and matter beyond all the power of man to count. In religious faith is found a well-spring of courage to fight on against all odds for the decencies of life. From religion stems the conviction that, as Dostoievsky said, "people are people and not the keys of a piano." Buttressed by religious faith, courage is able to transform obstacles into stepping stones, liabilities into assets, and adversity into a stairs whereon mankind can scale the heights of life's supreme achievements.

Summary

The best way to deal with adversity, afflictions and handicaps is to face them frankly, calmly, realistically. Study them carefully and see how they can be overcome, borne with patience, or transmuted into occasions for growth in mind, heart and soul. The fatal mistake is to seek to ignore them, to bury one's head in the sand. What matters is not what happens to an individual but how he reacts to those happenings. It is what he does to them that counts.

The frank facing of a menacing situation is the first step in removing its fangs. Thinking pays its richest dividends when done in the face of impending danger, adversity or actual affliction. Through facing the tribulation with clarity of vision, adherence to ideals and trust in God, the individual secures the courage to transmute adversity into a stairs on which to scale the heights.

RULE 8. *Face every adversity with calmness, study how to overcome it, convert it into a stepping stone to higher achievement; remember that what counts is not so much what happens to you as how you react to it.*

Reflect upon the instances of courage cited in this chapter and wait until tomorrow to read the next chapter.

CHAPTER NINE

THE COURAGE OF SAINTS

The Lord is my light and my salvation,
whom shall I fear?

—*Psalm* 26:1.

AN IMPORTANT INGREDIENT *in the courage that seeks to accomplish something of value is ideals. They supply motive power; they transform mere velleities into volitions: they perform a function similar to that of rods of steel in reinforced concrete. By focusing attention upon ideals, an individual secures strength for the second mile when the novelty of the first has passed.*

Adherence to ideals, however, implies faith in spiritual values which are rooted in a moral order. God is the author of the moral order which mirrors His nature and objectifies His thought. The moral order is immutable and eternal. An individual does not really break a moral law; he breaks himself upon the iron anvil of its unchanging validity.

God is the cosmic Underwriter of the moral order, the Guarantor of all spiritual values and the Vindicator of all ideals. In the clear perception of this mighty truth is to be found the secret of the courage of saints; their aim is to achieve the closest union with God. The perfect conformity of the human will with the will of God is the unfailing mark of high sanctity.

The consciousness of a saint that he is fulfilling God's law, is doing His will, fills his soul with a faith that moves mountains and a love that washes out fear. Why should he fear when he knows that he has God on his side?

"Love," says St. Paul, "is the fulfilling of the law." In the fulfillment of God's law, the saint finds his soul flooded with a peace that passeth understanding and with a love that embraceth even his enemies. "Perfect love," says St. John, "casteth out fear, because fear hath pain." Perfect love fills the soul and leaves no room for crippling fear or obsessing anxiety.

The technique of achieving the courage of saints is that of achieving their sanctity. In the proportion in which an individual achieves union with God in love and in service will he achieve freedom from anxiety and a high courage of soul that looks out into the faces of men through eyes that are unafraid. In fact, no lasting courage can be achieved except through a satisfactory philosophy of life based upon belief in God as the cosmic Underwriter of the moral order and the Vindicator of spiritual ideals and values.

The Most Courageous

Among the most courageous of all persons are the saints of God. They abound in moral courage which springs from a good conscience. The individual who makes his conduct conform to the law of God finds himself in union with its Author. In proportion to the closeness of that union does his courage mount: in proportion to the distance between the creature and the Creator does fear increase. Man does not lift himself up by his boot straps; he is raised up by the energizing strength which flows from the heart of God to all who cling to Him in love and service.

These are elementary truths in the spiritual life. They are familiar to all who have sought the comradeship of Christ by walking in His footsteps. No treatment of the iron virtue of courage would be at all complete if it did not penetrate to the deepest source of all courage—God Himself. He is the infinite well-spring whence flow the streams of valor, bravery, and daring which convert ordinary mortals of flesh and blood into saints and heroes.

What the sun is to plant life, God is to human life. Without the sun, vegetative life will soon wither and die. Without God, man becomes sickled o'er with fears and worries which rob him of his vitality, his initiative, his courage.

"He that followeth me," saith the Lord, "walketh not in darkness but shall have the light of life." And again: "I am the way, and the truth, and the life." Without the way there is no going; without the truth there is no knowing; without the life there is no living. Christ is the Light of the world. Face toward that Light and the shadows of disquietude and fear flee behind you.

That has been the experience of mankind throughout the centuries. When Cain hid from God, he took the one road to ever-increasing fear and dread; for the first time he heard the pensive music of a world out of tune. It is this cacophony which beats its wild crescendo in the ears of all who follow in his footsteps and fills them with a primaeval restlessness.

What Is a Saint?

What do we mean by a saint? An unattractive, lack-lustre person who rarely, if ever, smiles and who has little interest in his fellows? A joy-killer, solemn and dry, who is forever wearying people with his jeremiads about the vanities of the world and frightening them with his predictions of divine wrath? These seem to be the common conceptions. They are, however, caricatures which have little resemblance to the reality. They cause people to shy away from the ideal of sainthood because they find it so unappealing.

Contrary to this too prevalent misconception, a saint is the most attractive and likable of all people. He is filled with a constant love of God and of all His children; he is joyous, serene and considerate; in his veins runs the milk of human kindness. True, he retains his individual characteristics, for sanctity shines through the stained glass windows of human nature with its unending variations in temperament and personality.

Undoubtedly, the distinguishing mark of eminent holiness is an all-embracing love which harbors no resentments and knows no grudges. In the countenances of all men—white, black, yellow, brown—it sees the lineaments of the face of Christ. Sanctity means putting into practice the implications of the mighty truths of the Fatherhood of God and the brotherhood of man. The supreme joy in life is the quest of sainthood; the supreme tragedy is the loss of it.

No truth needs to be driven home more urgently than the real nature of sanctity. The widespread impression that a saint is some kind of a queer individual who holds himself aloof from the interests and joys of human life and radiates gloom has undoubtedly alienated the ideal of sainthood from many peole. It is time to point out that healthy common sense, cheerfulness, kindliness, courage and unfailing love are the authentic marks of sainthood. In fact, saintliness may be defined simply as common sense raised to the *nth* degree. There is no pathology in genuine holiness but only in its masquerade.

A Hierarchy of Values

Saints are invariably men and women of outstanding courage. Why? Because they keep close to the source of all courage, God Himself. They do this because they have worked out a coherent scheme of values which is the essence of a philosophy of life. The failure of many lives is traceable to the neglect to establish a rational hierarchy of values and to make their actions conform to that scale.

With the saints, the hierarchy or ascending scale of values is clearly defined. There are things of physical value; they minister to the needs of the body and the pleasures of the senses. They are not to be depreciated, but their limits are marked. The mistake which many worldlings make is to esteem them objects of supreme value, the goals of their life-long striving. The inevitable end of such a quest is dust and ashes.

Of higher value are the things which minister to the mind of man. As the mind is superior to the body, the things which conduce to growth and development of the mind rank above the objects of physical value. The search for beauty and truth distinguishes *homo sapiens* from the brute animals which never rise higher than the pursuit of food and drink and the satisfaction of the physical appetites. Knowledge, beauty, truth, wisdom are the objectives of man's long intellectual quest. While they are intangible and are unamenable to measuring by any mechanical measuring rods and scales, they are of enormous importance in enabling a man to be truly human, to live in that region of the mind and imagination whither the brutes never enter.

Higher still in the scale of values are those which minister to man's spiritual growth and progress. Justice, righteousness, mercy, honor, love—who will weigh their worth or set limits to their value? The achievement of these ethical values renders man a being of unique and transcendental worth. They make his face shine with a divine radiance and with a glory brighter than that of setting suns. It is the possession of these spiritual values which make a man God-like—the human image of the Divine.

Life presents a miscellany of values. The person who is to achieve integration of character must single out the highest and commit himself to them through thick and thin. He cannot espouse them all, but must learn to put first things first; the initial task in the forming of a philosophy of life is, therefore, that of selection. "The seeker of his truest, strongest, deepest self," points out William James, "must review the list carefully, and pick out the one on which to stake his salvation." It is upon the validity of the spiritual values that the saint stakes his all.

A friend once wrote to the Russian novelist, Ivan Turgenev: "It seems to me that to put oneself in the second place is the whole signficance of life." Turgenev thought otherwise. "It seems to me," he replied, *"to discover what to put before oneself,* in the first place, is the whole problem of life."

Christ is the Being whom all the saints put before themselves. They commit themselves without reserve to the spiritual values which were embodied in their fullness in His ministry of redemptive love and sacrificial service for mankind. It is loyalty to Christ that pulls the trigger of the energy of their minds and hearts and souls, issuing in deeds of kindliness and love. Surrendering himself to the Highest, the prayer of every saint is:

Make me a captive, Lord,
And then I shall be free;
Force me to render up my sword,
And I shall conq'ror be.

It is the distinction of saints that they not only profess such a hierarchical code of values, but also translate it into action. They organize the mob of conflicting appetites into orderly battalions which respect the commands of superiors. With saints there is no disparagement of physical and intellectual goods. There is, however, a refusal to sacrifice a spiritual good for either of these, and an unwavering insistence upon the sovereignty of the spiritual.

That is why martyrs, before going forth to the arena, the swordsman's block or the fire, were able to say with deadly earnestness to their followers: "Fear not those who can destroy only the body. Fear God alone. For only He has dominion over both body and soul." The life of every saint illustrates the truth of Professor Alfred Whitehead's observation: "True courage is not the brutal force of vulgar heroes, but the firm resolve of virtue and reason."

The Challenge to St. Augustine

Though St. Augustine had for some years past given theoretical assent to such a hierarchy of values, he had not been able to put it into practice. His conversion signalizes his emancipation from the chains of physical passion and the pride of intellect. His story of his emancipation is an epic in will power and in courage. His two wills, "one old, one new," he wrote, "one of the spirit, one of the flesh, fought angrily together, and my soul was on the rack."

A companion read the *Life of St. Anthony* to him. "Thou, Lord," continues St. Augustine, "in his words wast twisting me back to myself . . . wast setting me before my own face, that I might see how foul I was, how distorted and filthy, how soiled and ulcered. And if I tried to turn my gaze from myself, the reader went on reading, and thou didst thrust myself once more before my own eyes . . . till I lay naked to myself . . . and I kept saying: Let it be now! Let it be now! And as I spoke, I made towards the resolve, and I would stand still hard by, and draw breath. And again I would try . . . and all but—all but, I reached and I held; and lo, I was not there . . . Those vanities, my loves of yore, kept plucking softly at my robe of flesh, and softly whispering—Wilt thou dismiss us? and from this moment shall not this and that be allowed to thee any more for ever?"

On the other side there seemed to stand the army of the chaste, the strong, saying: "What these can do, cannot you?" The words continued to haunt him. Then, one day as he sat in his garden, with the inner conflict still raging, he heard a child's voice singing some nursery rhyme: *"Take it, read it; take it, read it."* Opening the Scripture, he read: "Not in riotings and drunkenness and impurities, but put you on the Lord Jesus Christ, and make no provision for the flesh and its lusts."

Here, then, was the challenge. Would he be courageous enough to accept it? His smoldering courage rose to a mighty flame as he seized the gauntlet flung down to him. His decision was made, his course was set, as he left that garden. He was to become a towering hero in the vanguard of the Lord and make Africa fragrant with the sweet odor of his virtue. What a new complexion courage puts on every situation in life!

St. Francis Xavier

Consider the role that courage played in the life of St. Francis Xavier. Born of a noble family and accustomed to the comforts of the wealthy, Francis answered the plea for missionaries to the Orient. Sailing from Lisbon in April, 1539, he did not reach India till May of the next year, after a ghastly voyage. The emigrants on the boat were the very scum of Portugal; for these rude, profane and panic-stricken people, Francis, though sick himself, sacrificed all —his food, his clothing, his cabin.

With indefatigable zeal he labored among the natives of Goa, India, sharing their meagre food and primitive conditions of living. He brought the tidings of Christ's Gospel to laborers at the Paravar pearl fisheries and exemplified those teachings in his own life. From 1542 to 1544, Francis made the 600-mile journey to Cape Comorin and back thirteen times. He moved in a world of dysentery, malaria, elephantiasis, enduring every hardship with a smile. So effective were his labors that some 30,000 converts were won for Christ by 1545. Thence he carried the banner of Christ to Ceylon, to sensuous Malacca, to the "Spice Islands" west of New Guinea, to the Papuan natives, to the head-hunters of Borneo, to the cannibals of Ceram and to the superstitious pagans in the Moluccas.

Worn out by his long traveling, thrice shipwrecked, attacked by Mohammedans, hiding in the bush, he was often starving. Did he complain or whisper about his hard lot, his torturing isolation from the cultured companions of his European homeland?

"Never," he wrote, *"have I been happier elsewhere, nor more continuously."*

The intimate companionship of Christ transmuted all these sufferings into joy and kindled a courage that quailed before no odds. "Who is there who can hurt you," he was accustomed to ask in the words of St. Paul, "if you be zealous of good?" Here is the transparent source of that flaming courage which wrote the name of Christ high in the skies of the Orient and deeper still in the hearts of its children.

Francis was not yet ready, however, to rest upon his oars. There were the islands of Japan which still remained to be converted. With meticulous care he prepared for that conquest: he studied the language, translated St. Matthew's Gospel into Japanese, and learned it by heart. Then, like a modern Godfrey de Bouillon advancing to attack a Saracen stronghold, Francis marched on single-handed for the conquest of the Land of the Rising Sun. So deeply did he plant the faith of Christ in the hearts of the Nipponese that neither the attrition of four centuries of circumambient paganism nor the persecution of Shinto emperors has been able to eradicate that ancient Christian colony.

A Symbol of Courage

There still loomed before Francis, however, the land of China with its teeming millions. How ardently Francis yearned to bring to them the life-giving Gospel of Christ! In 1552 he at last sailed for China, but was able to reach only the island of Sancian off the coast of the Chinese mainland. Sick with fever and attacked by shivering fits, he grew weaker.

"Shall I reach China?" he wrote. "I do not know. Everything is against it."

Alone with a Malabar servant and a Chinese boy, he became worse. Though bled and re-bled, he passed into delirium; he now reverted to the language of his childhood, Basque. Constantly on his lips was the name he loved most of all—the Name of Jesus. Under his black cassock were the signatures of his dear friends in distant Spain and Rome, signatures he had cut from their letters, and which, along with a copy of the vows he had made to Christ, he wore next to his heart.

My friend, Father Charles C. Martindale, S.J., of Oxford, sketches thus vividly the deathbed scene of this bold warrior for Christ: "Imagine a mere framework of a hut, the palm-leaf thatch in fragments; the wind, setting the little lamp flaring and flickering; the ceaseless sound of waves; the Crucifix fastened up by the Chinaman, with China invisible behind it, and the white face and shining eyes of Francis, who was all but speechless now, seeing nothing but the Crucifix, the memorial of Christ and of His death. Now were the maps rolled up; now was the traveling done with. Now was Ignatius, far away at his desk in Rome, now was even he bidden a last farewell. Now was the thrill of Paris, and now was the home in Spain—since which he had known no home—handed over to God, and left there. 'Into Thy hand' I commend it all; my life and my eternity. The night of December 2 passed by. Only the Chinaman watched by the dying Saint. At 2 o'clock on the 3rd, when the winds and the waters grew restless, Francis, too, stirred. The unmistakable and ultimate change touched him. The vigilant native rose, put a lighted candle into the hand of Francis, and held it there. Perhaps, in the breeze of the day, it expired. But at that same hour, all alone, save for the Chinaman and the companionship of Christ Crucified, Francis Xavier died." *

Probably no other man since the days of St. Paul won so many souls for Christ as did this dauntless soldier of the Lord. Despite the lapse of nearly four centuries, Christians at Goa, Travancore, Ceylon, Mailapur, Japan and in the islands of the Malay archipelago still thrill at the

* *What Are Saints?* New York and London, Sheed & Ward, pp.95-96.

mention of his name. His coffin at Goa shows that he was small in stature, being only about five feet, but he had the courage of a giant. With St. Paul he was able to say: "In all things we suffer tribulation, but are not distressed; we are straitened, but are not destitute." With the Palmist, too, he could say: "Though I should walk in the midst of the shadow of death, I will fear no evil, for Thou art with me." Soldier of peace, athlete of God, conqueror of the Orient for Christ, St. Francis Xavier stands as a symbol of a courage that never waned in the doing of gallant deeds of service for the divine Master.

Apostle of Negro Slaves

The great apostle of Negro slaves is St. Peter Claver. Graduating from the University of Barcelona, Peter decided to devote his life to the service of the Lord. Learning the sad plight of the slaves, Peter cast his lot with them. In 1610 he landed at Cartagena, where for forty-four years he was the servant and the protector of the unfortunate blacks who were torn away from their homes in Africa to be beasts of burden for the white man.

Early in the seventeenth century the masters of Central and South America needed laborers to cultivate the soil and exploit the gold mines. The coasts of Guinea, the Congo and Angola became the market for slave dealers; to these traffickers petty kings sold their subjects and their prisoners. Because of its position in the Caribbean Sea, Cartagena became the chief slave mart of the New World.

Each month saw a thousand or more brought to its port. The slaves were bought for a dollar, and sold for 200.

Even though half the cargo might die, the traffic remained enormously profitable. Neither the censures of the pope nor the protests of churchmen could prevail against the greed of the merchants. Unable to suppress the vile traffic the missionaries strove to alleviate it.

Foremost among them was Peter Claver. He met each boat and took the fear-crazed slaves under his special care. Their condition was pitiable in the extreme. They had been packed in bundles of six, with chains around their necks and ankles, wedged under decks where no sunshine ever came, in a stench into which no white officer would put his head for fear of fainting. Once a day they would be given water and maize. They were called "black cattle" and treated as such.

When they arrived, they were covered with sores, vermin and filth. Frantically homesick, half-crazed by fear because of the brutal way in which they were treated, and terror-stricken at the prospect of worse evils in store for them, they were indeed objects of pity. Despite their awful stench, Peter washed them, dressed their sores, made beds for them, clothed them, spoke words of kindness to them. Beneath the repulsive countenance of each, Peter saw the lineaments of the gentle face of Christ, and he caught an echo of the divine voice whispering: "Amen I say to you, as long as you did it to one of these, my least brethren, you did it to me." If each of them had been a king, Peter could not have been kinder to them.

His solicitude was not limited to their physical needs, but embraced their spiritual wants as well. He instructed them in the teachings of Christ and baptized them. He inquired of the needs of each and defended them against their oppressors. He visited the villages into which the slaves had been sent, so that he might continue to minister to them and to curb any brutality on the part of their masters.

Opposition came not only from slave traders but also from so-called Christians who thought Peter profaned the sacraments by administering them to these "black cattle" who scarcely possessed a soul. Fashionable women of Cartagena refused to enter the churches where Peter conducted services for the slaves. Thus was he caught between the fire of the greedy slave merchants and that of influential members of the Christian community.

Here, a strange thing happened. Peter had been of a timid and non-assertive nature, but now that danger was threatening his flock, his latent courage rose to a flame. Manfully did he stand his ground and continue to blaze a new trail of kindliness and mercy for the downtrodden and enslaved black man. Engaging in no recrimination, bearing his humiliations patiently, Peter worked harder than ever, if that were possible, to win for them, in the eyes of all, the essential dignity of human personalities, made in the image of God. If that basic truth could be driven home to the conscience of all Christians, Peter knew that its implications would inevitably trace themselves out in the amelioration of their lot and in their eventual emancipation. In his long ministry among them, he is said to have baptized more than 300,000 slaves, raising them to the dignity of children of God and heirs of Heaven.

A Slave Made King

In addition to ministering to the Negro slaves, Peter also labored for those other afflicted creatures, the lepers at St. Lazarus. Thither he would bring lint, bandages, ointments, material for mosquito curtains. He would assist in the dressing of their sores, and the mantle of his cassock he was continually giving as a robe for the leprous, a veil for lupus-gnawed faces, and a pillow for the dying.

From the hospital Peter went to the prisons. He would visit each inmate and say a word of mercy and hope. He made it a custom to be with the condemned man at the time of execution, and also sought to reconcile him beforehand with his God. When the rope would occasionaly break, he would take the shrieking victim in his arms and hold him to his heart.

Toward the end of his life, he was so worn out and exhausted from his ceaseless labors that he had to be *strapped to his horse* to make his rounds of the harbor, prison and leper house. The bottom edge of his cassock was always in rags, as the slaves, prisoners and lepers insisted on tearing shreds from it, and venerated them as relics.

Sometimes, when a mob of the Negroes were running amok, Peter would be sent for in haste, and his very presence would quell the riot. When an entire population was fleeing from the vicinity of a volcano, he sent them a message to remain there till he arrived the next day. They did so. Then he led the Negroes, still quivering with panic, around the still active crater and planted a cross on its lips. No one was hurt. "The hesitating youth," says his biographer, "had become the indomitable man, and walked serene along the very razor-edge of peril."

When news of his death on September 8, 1654, spread throughout the city, the people rushed in throngs to his home. There he lay, holding still in his clenched hand his little picture of the lay brother, Alphonsus Rodriguez, who first told him of the crying needs of the West Indies missions. It was Peter's way of saying thanks to the humble door-keeper at Majorca for pointing to a field so ripe for service to the most unfortunate of all God's creatures.

Then children filled the streets, refusing to move, calling for "St. Peter Claver." Then a new army assembled. It was that of the Negroes who pushed their way through all the throngs and broke through the guard at the door to gaze for the last time upon the face of their shepherd and their defender, dearer to them than all the world.

They stooped and kissed the floor of the room that held his body, so sure were they that he was a man filled full of God, and was now His saint. No king expiring upon the silken cushions of his regal bed ever left such emptiness in the hearts of his subjects as did Peter Claver in the hearts of the slaves, the prisoners, and the lepers of Cartagena. He had declared himself "the slave of the Negroes forever." They made him their uncrowned king.

Peter Claver felled no enemy with his sword, struck no one—even when abused, he did not strike back—yet his life was filled with courageous deeds. It was not mere sentiment that brought him hurrying to meet each shipload of slaves. It was courage and love. So dreadful was the ordeal of washing and caring for them that, when the tolling bell sounded the arrival of a new ship, Peter would break out in cold sweat as he remembered the previous experience. Yet, back and back and back again he went for forty-four years. There is the courage which rested for its support, not upon flying banners nor martial airs, nor the plaudits of cheering multitudes, but upon the principle of the nobility of service to the downtrodden and the afflicted, done in the name of Jesus.

It was the courage of loving these "cattle" with all his heart, mind, soul and strength. It was the courage of fulfilling Christ's law of love when it was most difficult to do so. For an ounce of courage that springs from hate, a ton flows from the mighty well-spring of love. Love transformed a hesitant, timid youth into a bold and gallant servant of God, who blazed new trails through the dank, dark jungles of our prejudice and greed, trails which lead to the dawning of a new day of social altruism and human brotherhood.

"Love Casteth out Fear"

More and more, psychologists, psychiatrists, psychoanalysts and all who deal with the problems of human behavior are coming to recognize the supreme service of love in washing away the multitudinous mental quirks and complexes which fear breeds. Love achieves the simplest and the most effective catharsis of all such phobias. It builds self-confidence and courage.

Writing not as a moralist but as a good psychologist,

William James observed: "Love your enemies! Mark you, not simply those who happen not to be your friends, but your enemies, your positive and active enemies. Either this is a mere Oriental hyperbole, a bit of verbal extravagance, meaning only that we should, as far as we can, abate our animosities, or else it is sincere and literal. Outside of certain cases of intimate individual relation, it seldom has been taken literally. Yet it makes one ask the question: Can there in general be a level of emotion so unifying, so obliterative of differences between man and man, that even enmity may come to be an irrelevant circumstance and fail to inhibit the friendlier interest aroused? If positive well-wishing could attain so supreme a degree of excitement, those who were swayed by it might well seem superhuman beings. Their life would be morally discrete from the life of other men, and there is no saying . . . what the effects might be; they might conceivably transform the world." * Saints like Peter Claver have played their part in transforming the slavery-approving civilization of the seventeenth century to one that finds it abhorrent in every way.

Saints are people whose dominant motivation is not fear, but love. That love extends to all mankind, even to one's enemies. Love dries up the pus pockets of hatred and cauterizes them with deeds of kindly service. "There is no fear in love," says St. John, the beloved disciple of Our Lord, "but perfect love casteth out fear, for fear hath pain." In that brief utterance St. John has expressed a profound psychological truth whose therapeutic implications

* *The Varieties of Religious Experience,* p. 283.

psychiatrists will be unraveling to the end of time. The best way, both morally and psychologically, to overcome one's enemies is to love them. Lincoln perceived this truth and practised it.

At a dinner in Washington, he spoke kindly and even in endearing terms of some of the Confederates.

"I am surprised, Mr. President," said an elderly lady nearby, "to hear you speak of our enemies in such a kind way. I should think you would seek to destroy them instead of trying to love them."

"But do I not destroy them as enemies," replied Lincoln, "when I make them our friends?"

Such a procedure is not only good Christianity, but good statesmanship as well.

Love rejoices in the excellence of others and wishes them well. Jealousy is a perversion of that capacity, twisting the sensitiveness of the other's superiority from its legitimate path of rejoicing into the pathological tangents of petulance, peevishness, anger, fear. "Against the superiority of another," said Goethe, "the only remedy is love."

Love enables one to open wide his eyes to another's excellence, to admire and rejoice in it, and thus to enrich himself through his frank recognition. He shares through appreciation in that excellence. Excellence in others, like great works of art, enriches all who view them with admiration. The saints, with their supreme capacity for loving all mankind and scorning all temptatitons toward pettiness, envy or selfishness, are thus like the immortal works of art which enrich every generation which opens its eyes to their beauty.

Faith Breeds Courage

The saints are people of great faith. God and the invisible realities of the spiritual world are more vivid and real to them than the material objects which impinge upon their senses. They are not bitten by doubts which paralyze the nerves of action nor palsied with questionings which transform forthright conduct into endless vacillations. They are not fissured personalities, but well-balanced, integrated ones. They know where they are going and how to get there. They are willing to face opposition and endure hardship and suffering to achieve their goal. They know that, as long as they have God on their side, they cannot lose—for God and one constitute a majority.

In thus affording one a consciousness of the presence of God, religious faith is a source of courage. The doubter, the sceptic, is exposed to a devastating sense of loneliness and isolation. He feels like a sequestered being in an alien world. "How lonely we are," observes Thackeray, "in the world! how selfish and secret! everybody! . . . Ah, sir,—a distinct universe walks about under your hat and under mine—all things in nature are different to each—the woman we look at has not the same features, the dish we eat from has not the same taste to the one and the other—you and I are but a pair of infinite isolations, with some fellow-islands a little more or less near to us."

While this feeling of isolation may come at times to everyone, it is the sceptic who is particularly haunted with this sense of cosmic loneliness. To the believer, dark skies and rainy days may come, but he knows they will pass and soon the sun will shine again. He is at home in His Father's vast temple and knows that he can never wander beyond the reach of His everlasting arms.

The Maid of Orleans

St. Joan of Arc offers a striking illustration of the courage that springs from a deep religious faith, and from faith in the mission which she believed to have been entrusted to her by God. A simple, peasant girl rides forth to drive the English from Orleans and to crown the dauphin, Charles, king of France. In February, 1429, accompanied by six-men-at-arms, she sets forth on her perilous mission to the court of the dauphin at Chinon. Her calm assurance of the success of her mission overcomes the doubts of Charles, who outfits for her an army of about 5,000 men.

Clothed with a coat of mail, armed with the sword with which Charles Martel had vanquished the Saracens, she rides at the head of the army. She inspires them with her confidence and fearlessness and leads them to a brilliant victory at Orleans, forcing the English to flee. All are agreed that the victory was traceable chiefly to Joan's extraordinary pluck and daring leadership.

In a single week, with victories at Jargeau, Beaugency and Batay, the English were driven beyond the Loire. Joan had now made it possible to crown Charles the King of France. On July 17, 1429, holding the sacred banner, she stood beside Charles at his coronation in the cathedral of Rheims. In an unbelievably short time, Joan's courage and determination had achieved the impossible.

Neither did her pluck and bravery desert her when, her mission accomplished, tribulation fell like rain upon her. Condemned as a heretic and a witch, and about to be burned at the stake in the street of Rouen, she displayed the same calm demeanor, the same fearless scorn of danger. Even when the flames mounted around her, there were no shrieking cries, no agonized pleading for release from the fiery death meted out to her by the people whose country she had freed and whose monarch she had crowned. Here was a courage which eclipsed even her spectacular victory at Orleans. "Courage in strife," observes H. M. Tomlinson, "is common enough; even the dogs have it. But the courage which can face the ultimate defeat of a life of good will . . . that is different, that is victory."

To the people of France, St. Joan of Arc is a symbol of the twin virtues of patriotism and religion, the love of country and the love of God. In travels through France, I have found few, if any, statues of popular heroes so ubiquitous in town and countryside as that of the Maid of Orleans with her sword held high. To me, she stands as a symbol of courage in victory and in defeat. As Browning says:

> *. . . Through such souls alone,*
> *God, stooping, shows sufficient of His light*
> *For us in the dark to rise by. And I rise.*

Calmness and Faith

The life of every saint illustrates the truth that religious faith begets calmness and courage. When the Apostles awakened Christ, fearful that the storm at sea would capsize their frail bark, Christ laid bare the source of their fear when He said: "Why are you fearful, *O ye of little faith?*" Why are you so foolish as to fear, the Master asks, when you know that I am with you? Religious faith washes away fear and begets an inner steadiness upon which the outward blows of adversity beat in vain.

When faith collapses, the dyke of courage is broken and fears sweep through the soul like tidal waves. "An atheist," observes John Buchan, "is a man who has no invisible means of support." He is like a weathervane, at the mercy of every wind that blows. Psychiatrists are pointing out in increasing numbers the value of a deep religious faith in serving as an anchor to the windward.

"A man," says Robert Louis Stevenson, "should stop his ears against paralysing terror, and run the race that is set before him with a single mind." That is precisely what religion helps a man to do. "The sovereign cure for worry," observes William James, "is religious faith. It supplies motive power for action and the enthusiasm which commits the whole man, mind and heart and soul, to the undertaking." Says Oliver Wendell Holmes: "It's faith in something and enthusiasm that makes life worth looking at."

The weakness of Freud's position is that he expected man to handle by his own unaided will the disruptive forces of his subconscious life. "Freud has unfortunately overlooked," Jung points out, "the fact that man has never yet been able single-handed to hold his own against the powers of darkness—that is, of the unconscious. Man has always stood in need of the spiritual help which each individual's own religion held out to him. . . .It is this which lifts him out of his distress." *

The Power of Prayer

There is another powerful factor, operative in the lives of saints, which vivifies the sense of the divine presence and enhances their courage. That factor is prayer. Prayer means essentially the drawing closer to God by raising our mind to Him in adoration and supplication and opening one's heart to Him in love. God is the source of all strength and courage. It is not possible to come closer to that divine Source without feeling the impact of His strength and courage upon one's soul. No one ever falls upon his knees in prayer without rising a better and stronger man.

Above the doors of the Church of Our Lady of Guadalupe in Cuernavaca, Mexico, I read the simple inscription: *Entra bueno, sal mejor* — Enter a good person, leave a better one. Though the first part of the injunction may not always be observed, the latter always is. Tennyson recognized the mighty and all pervasive power of prayer when he makes his hero, the dying King Arthur, say:

More things are wrought by prayer
Than this world dreams of.

No less an authority than Dr. Alexis Carrel has recently borne witness to the power of prayer in overcoming phobias, melancholy and other complexes. "As a physician," he states, "I have seen men, after all other therapy

* *Modern Man in Search of a Soul,* pp. 277, 278.

had failed, lifted out of disease and melancholy by the serene effort of prayer. It is the only power in the world that seems to overcome the so-called 'laws of nature'; the occasions on which prayer has dramatically done this have been termed 'miracles.' But a constant, quieter miracle takes place hourly in the hearts of men and women who have discovered that prayer supplies them with a steady flow of sustaining power in their daily lives. When we pray, we link ourselves with the inexhaustible motive power that spins the universe. We ask that a part of this power be apportioned to our needs. Even in asking, our human deficiencies are filled and we arise strengthened and repaired." *

Because the saints were men and women of prayer, they possessed great courage. Christ set the example for all of us: before entering upon His passion and death, He retired to the Garden of Gethsemani to engage in long and fervent prayer. When He found the Apostles, Peter, James and John, who had accompanied Him, fallen asleep, He awakened them, saying: "What? Could you not watch one hour with me? Watch ye and pray." Arising from those hours of prayer in the Garden, Christ went through the scourgings, the sufferings, and the death upon Calvary's gibbet with a courage which is an inspiration to all men and women who must bear a cross and suffer.

A Troubador of Christ

Among the most gentle and lovable of all the saints of God is Francis of Assisi. He has captured the hearts

* *The Readers' Digest,* March 1941, p. 34.

of all the world. Even those of no faith turn wistful eyes toward this troubador of Christ, whose love for everything in nature, animate and inanimate, made him a minstrel singing always the praises of God. Yet a careful study of his life discloses that, with all his cheerfulness and mirth, he was among the most fearless of all. His love for everything and everyone seems to have washed every trace of fear from his soul. He offers a perfect illustration of the truth of St. John's words: "There is no fear in love."

As a youth, he was a fastidious dresser, a courtier of pleasure, a suitor of beauty, eager for fun and merriment. He was actually crowned as the king of revelers. As he was riding across the Umbrian plain, he met a leper begging alms. Francis had always had a special horror of lepers. Putting the spurs into his horse, he turned his face away to escape from the repulsive sight. Then, quickly, he caught the echo of a voice whispering: "Amen I say to you, as long as you did it not to one of these least, neither did you do it to me." Reining in his steed, he returned, and dismounted. Taking all the money he had, he gave it to the beggar and kissed him.

It was the most difficult thing Francis had ever done; but it marked the changing point in his life. He had found his client and his life work. Henceforth, he renounced all riches that he might dedicate himself to the lepers, the sick, and the ragged poor. His bride henceforth was Lady Poverty; even the clothes on his back he surrendered. With a cloak given to him by the Bishop of Assisi, he went off into the woods of Mount Subasio, singing for joy.

All the things of nature—the wind, the sun, the sky, the flowers, grass and trees, the birds and beasts of the field—were his possessions now, his "brothers and sisters," and God was his treasure supreme.

His love for poverty has probably never been surpassed. I saw in the church at Assisi a lovely fresco by Giotto, depicting the "holy nuptials of Francis with Lady Poverty." It has been the theme of a thousand poets, sculptors and painters who find their imagination stirred by a wedding to so unusual a bride. It was because Francis had the courage to try to walk so faithfully in the footsteps of Him who did not have whereupon to lay His head that he had so great a devotion to poverty. The secret of this love which, while provoking their admiration, has mystified so many, is revealed in the following beautiful prayer which he addressed to his Lord:

"Poverty was in the crib and like a faithful squire she kept herself armed in the great combat Thou didst wage for our redemption. During Thy passion she alone did not forsake Thee. Mary, Thy Mother, stopped at the foot of the Cross, but poverty mounted it with Thee and clasped Thee in her embrace unto the end; and when Thou was dying of thirst, as a watchful spouse she prepared for Thee the gall. Thou didst expire in the ardour of her embraces, nor did she leave Thee when dead, O Lord Jesus, for she allowed not Thy body to rest elsewhere than in a borrowed grave. O poorest Jesus, the grace I beg of Thee is to bestow on me the treasure of the highest poverty. Grant that the distinctive mark of our Order may be never to possess as its own anything under the sun, for the glory of Thy Name, and to have no other patrimony than begging."

In this ardent love of poverty one finds the keynote of the spirit of the Poverello and of the Order which he founded. Does it take courage to give up every earthly possession and to live a life of poverty till mother earth at last loans you six feet of empty space? Try it, and see.

"A God-intoxicated Man"

While Francis was gentle to others, like all the saints, he was severe upon himself. Self-denial was his daily food and mortification his close-fitting garment. So severe was he with his body that, when he came to die, he begged pardon of "brother Ass the body" for having treated it with such scant courtesy. Yet, instead of his mortification making him gloomy or irritable, it heightened his cheerfulness and deepened his joy. His early love of song never waned, and during his last illness he spent much of his time in singing—a God-intoxicated man if there ever was one. His love of God and of all His creatures flowed from him in words so tender that they seem like lyrics of love. Let me cite the prayer that was almost hourly on his lips, and ask if there exists, in all the literature of the world, a prayer more beautiful.

"Lord," prayed Francis, "make me an instrument of Thy peace; where there is hatred, let me sow love; where there is injury, pardon; where there is doubt, faith; where there is despair, hope; where there is sadness, joy.

"O Divine Master, grant that I may not so much seek to be consoled as to console; to be understood as to understand; to be loved as to love; for it is in giving that we receive, it is in pardoning that we are pardoned, and it is in dying that we are born to eternal life."

Where will one find such pregnancy, such tenderness, such self-effacing love? Can one utter that without rising from his knees a better man? It is the unique contribution of Francis to show the world that the highest courage is achieved in the losing of oneself in the love of God and in the service of His children. He who gains the victory over himself achieves the supreme triumph; he who empties himself in love and service to the downtrodden, the afflicted and the ragged poor fills himself to the overflowing with joy and gladness.

Francis traced out in his daily life the implications of the amazing paradox that one begins to live only when he forgets himself in his absorption for the welfare of others. Beneath the soft and gentle music of social altruism and unselfish service, the ear, sensitive to the overtones, will not fail to detect those coming ever and anon from the iron chord of courage—the courage of self-conquest, the courage of joyous service, the courage of self-effacing love.

No soldier with helmet and loaded gun ever showed greater fearlessness than Francis. In 1212, he set out to preach the Gospel to the Saracens. His vessel was wrecked, however, and he was compelled to return. After preaching in the towns and the countryside of Italy, Francis once again set out for the East. He made his way to Egypt, where Damietta was under seige by the Crusaders. Francis was not unaware of the treatment meted out by the Sultan to those who fell within his hands; yet he deliberately gave himself up as a prisoner that he might be taken before this ruler. Standing fearlessly before the mighty warrior, Francis openly preached the Gospel of Christ.

Probably never before in the history of the world had quite such an incident taken place. There was in Francis an intrepidity, a complete indifference about his own safety, that made the sultan see at once that here was no ordinary man. Overcome with wonderment and awe at the strange spectacle, the sultan sent him back safely to the Christian camp. The words of Milton in *Samson Agonsites* depicts the courage of Francis, who

> *Ran on embattled armies clad in iron,*
> *And, weaponless himself,*
> *Made arms ridiculous.*

Francis sounded all the notes in the diapason of courage. From the lowest, a disregard of his physical safety, to the highest, when he kissed the hand of the leprous beggar and emptied himself in love and service to the poor and lowly, the Poverello of Assisi went all the way. Francis showed that gentleness, tenderness, and love have an underlining of the iron virtue. The Franciscan Order, which encircles the globe like a beautiful rosary of self-effacing charity, is the lengthened shadow of the personality of its Christlike founder. True to the injunctions of its founder, it will be found not among the rich and powerful, but among the poor, the afflicted, the lowly. For these were the clients of Francis and they are still the clients of his Order and the objects of their special predilection.

No more authentic expression of the spirit of Christ's courage and love will be found in the world today.

"Not I—But Christ"

Most men shrink from suffering and death. Yet, with the example of Christ before his eyes, St. Peter had the courage not only to face his executioners calmly but also to request them to crucify him head downwards, saying that he was not worthy to be crucified after the manner of His Lord. The vast legion of men and women who died as martyrs for their Christian faith demonstrate that there is no power in the external world which can crush the naked soul of man when vivified by a deathless faith and an invincible will. All the saints and heroes and martyrs of the race are monuments of courage against which time is both toothless and scytheless.

St. Paul offers a good illustration of the transforming power of religious faith and prayer. From a persecutor of the Christians he was changed into one of the most tireless propagators of the faith that ever lived. He braved all the perils of the ancient world and all the craftiness of man in his burning zeal to extend the kingdom of God on earth. He had become a God-intoxicated man. With truth was he able to say: "We preach not ourselves, but Jesus Christ our Lord." In telling of his many vicissitudes, he is quick to tell also of the courage which streamed from Christ to sustain him.

"In all things," he says, "we suffer tribulations, but are not distressed; we are straitened, but are not destitute; we suffer persecution, but are not forsaken; we are cast down, but we perish not; always bearing about in our body the mortification of Jesus, that the life also of Jesus may be made manifest in our bodies. For we who live are always delivered unto death for Jesus' sake; that the life also of Jesus may be made manifest in our mortal flesh."

Through all his external activities—traveling, preaching, writing—St. Paul had never suffered the inner life of prayer and communion with God to lapse. On the contrary, the intimacy of that union became intensified so that he was able to say: "And I live, now not I: but Christ liveth in men." Was it any wonder then that nothing could frighten nor scare him. Who could harm him? What power could hurt him?

"Who then," he said, "shall separate us from the love of Christ? Shall tribulations? or distress? or famine? or nakedness? or danger? or persecution? or the sword?. . . . But in all these things we overcome, because of Him that hath loved us. For I am sure that neither death, nor life, nor angels, nor principalities, nor powers, nor things present, nor things to come, nor might, nor height, nor depth, nor any other creature, shall be able to separate us from the love of God, which is in Christ Jesus our Lord."

While St. Paul placed a tremendous emphasis upon the duty of loving God, he did not fail to underline the duty of loving one's neighbor. Writing to the Galatians, he said: "For the whole law is fulfilled in one word. Thou shalt love thy neighbor as thyself. But if you bite and devour one another, take heed or you will be consumed by one another." Would that these words might be written in the skies of all the world. If they were but heeded by the nations, how many millions of young lives would be spared from a holocaust of fire?

When at last his long voyaging for Christ was finished, they led him out from his underground prison at Rome and gave him the opportunity he coveted of sealing his love for Christ with his life's blood. A half-dozen soldiers hurried him out down through the squalid slums of the Tiber; he turned his back to the theatres and palaces and temples of the Rome of Nero and went with the soldiers down the Ostian Way some three miles out. Then they turned off to the left into a little pine wood where a spring flowed. Old, sick, lonely, worn-out with his incessant traveling, Christ's servant was stripped and flogged for the last time. His body was bruised and bleeding, but his face was radiant as he placed his head upon the swordsman's block.

Separate him from Christ? How he must have smiled at the thought. Unwittingly they were going to confer upon the Apostle the favor he craved most of all. They were going to unite him with Christ, so that now he would reach the peak of that fulfillment of which he spoke: *"I live, now not I: but Christ liveth in me."*

These are the words that might well be carved upon the corner stone of the majestic temple, St. Paul-outside-the-Walls, which rises above his tomb into the skies of Rome. In teaching mankind the supreme importance of living for, in, and with Christ, St. Paul taught mankind the unfailing pathway that leads to a courage that fears no enemies and that never dies. Thousands of years ago the Psalmist declared: "The Lord is my light and my salvation, whom shall I fear?" That has been the Light by which the saints, prophets, and holy men and women of God in all ages have walked the paths of courage, righteousness and honor. Mankind, groping in the mists of uncertainty and doubt, will find that when they walk in that Light their vision becomes clearer, their footsteps surer, and in their hearts there echoes more steadily the music of the iron chord of courage.

Summary

Basic in the development of the highest courage is a belief in spiritual ideals and values. Saints have such a belief because they trace such values to the moral order whose Underwriter and Guarantor is God. Their constant aim is to secure union with God through conformity of their will tc His will in all things; such conformity is the unfailing mark of high sanctity. Futhermore, the fulfillment of God's will floods the soul with peace which washes away all anxiety.

It likewise fills the soul with love which embraces even one's enemies. Such perfect love cleanses the soul of fear. The technique of achieving the courage of saints is that of achieving their sanctity, their goodness, their love and their union with God. In fact, no permanent conquest of fear and anxiety can be achieved except through a satisfactory philosophy of life based on faith in God as the ultimate Vindicator of all spiritual ideals and values.

RULE 9. *Make it a point to strive constantly to cleanse your heart of the pus pockets of hate with a love for God and all men, even your enemies; thus do you achieve sanctity and union with God, and tap the wellspring of courage.*

Reflect upon the instances of courage cited in this chapter and wait until tomorrow to read the next chapter.

CHAPTER TEN

COURAGE FOR ALL

Perfect love casteth out fear,
because fear hath pain.

—*I John* 4:18

COURAGE IS NEEDED *not only by the soldier, the athlete, the scientist, the explorer, the statesman and the saint, but also by the ordinary man and woman who walk in the valley and perform the commonplace duties of life. The very fact that their work is done in obscurity, with no cheering multitudes to spur them on, subjects them to the temptation of thinking that their tasks are inconsequential and unimportant. Such an attitude is not conducive to the development of courage, but of timorous indifference and slipshod slovenliness.*

The remedy lies in the realization that the most ordinary work can be invested with a supreme dignity and a divine significance. That which can so transform the prosaic work of the home, the factory and the fields is the spirit in which it is done. In the eyes of God the spirit of dedication in which a task is performed is not less important than the task itself. Through the performance of commonplace duties supremely well and in a spirit of dedication, the humblest toiler can climb the golden ladder of consecrated labor to the throne of God.

The clear realization that we and our work are as precious in the eyes of God as are the kings and generals who stand in the limelight of the world's gaze is the tonic needed to hearten and inspirit all of us to invest our daily work with a divine significance and to fill our souls with a serene and lofty courage. It is the magic alchemy which transmutes the leaden dross of the commonplace into the shining gold of heroic achievement. It transforms timorous indifference into high courage.

Courage of the Commonplace

The courage of the soldier, the explorer, the hero, the martyr, is usually manifested in a dramatic and spectacular manner. Heroic feats are given the center of the stage; they are proclaimed in song and story; they are commemorated in the statues which adorn our public buildings and points of vantage in our cities. The spectacular and the dramatic find ready audiences and receive their meed of admiration and applause.

There is also the courage of the commonplace. The prosaic duties of the housewife, of the father of a family, of the merchant, done day by day, are not without their courage. The very fact that these duties are generally performed simply and quietly, with no blaring bands or cheering crowds, implies not less but more courage. This faithful, conscientious performance of daily duties, no matter how menial or how monotonous they may be, is always an expression of the iron virtue.

Fortitude and courage of a high order are found not so much in the doing of unusual deeds as in the doing of our daily tasks supremely well. It is the spirit with which our duties are performed that is of supreme importance. Tasks done grudgingly lose half of their value: duties performed with generous zeal and cheerful willingness are suffused with the radiance of nobility. It is this spirit which lifts the deed of humblest service from the valley of the ordinary to the mountain peaks of excellence. The pathway of heroes is trodden by all who discharge the duties of their station in life with high courage and fidelity.

The humble laborer, the mother, the merchant, the lawyer, the physician, can scale the heights of noble achievement by their devotion to duty not less successfully than those who do spectacular and unusual feats. The end for which they labor ennobles and sanctifies all their actions. "The meal and water," observes Ralph Waldo Emerson, "that are the commissariat of the soldiers of the *forlorn hope* that stake their lives to defend the pass are sacred as the Holy Grail." In the eyes of God, the most commonplace duties and the most menial tasks are clothed with the ermine of royalty.

St. Joseph, the saint of the commonplace, did nothing spectacular in his whole life. However, he did the simple tasks supremely well. In the mind of the Christian Church he occupies one of the high places in Heaven. He teaches all of us, whose lots are down in the valley, doing the prosaic tasks of life, that we, too, may achieve the highest courage and nobility of soul.

How can we achieve courage? How can we walk with the heroes of our race, despite the fact that we are destined to be apostles in the valley of the commonplace?

How can we conquer the fears which are making cowards of so many in the world today? Unless we know the methods for the conquest of fear, we can never achieve courage and serenity of soul.

The Conquest of Fear

Courage is more dependent upon mental attitudes, habits of thinking, methods of reacting emotionally, than upon external circumstance. Being an affair of the mind, it is assailed more by foes within than by enemies without. The chief of these internal foes is fear; it is the arch-enemy of our happiness, the darkest shadow that clouds the radiance of our joy. It assails us in early youth, dogs our footsteps through life and accompanies us to the grave. Unless fear is conquered or at least brought under reasonable restraint, there is little hope of abiding courage or happiness.

What sight is more pathetic than that of the frightened child for whom there are no loving arms to still the heart-quakings? What spectacle is sadder than that of the robust man shrinking and cowering from the ghosts of his own obsessing fear? Fear paralyzes life, robs the victim of the capacity for spontaneous laughter and joy, and causes him to limp through life's colorful scenes like a corpse at a wedding feast. "The thing in the world I am most afraid of," says Montaigne, "is fear, and with good reason, since that passion in the trouble it causes exceeds all accidents."

Fear is no respecter of persons, but assaults the high and the lowly, the rich and the poor, the educated and the ignorant. "The bondage of fear," observes Hugh Black, "has been the weariest slavery of the race. Fear entered Eden when sin entered, and fear has gripped man and held him in spiritual tyranny. Men have been afraid of life and of death, afraid of today and of tomorrow, afraid of the living and of the dead, afraid of man and of God, afraid of everything and of nothing."

While education has banished certain of the fears which sprang from superstitions of the past, the very complexity of modern civilization seems to have begotten a new brood of phobias. Fear stalks through our land today, hurling defiance at the "G" men to capture it. Like the dragon in old legends, it seizes its victims by the thousands and drags them off to its gloomy lair to prey upon them. It is no wonder that our nerves are jumpy, and the people are scared half-stiff with worry and dread. Indeed, medical authorities inform us that worry, directly or indirectly, takes a larger annual toll of human life than any other disease. It is scarcely too much to assert that, if fear were abolished from modern life, the work of the psychotherapist would be nearly gone.

What help does religion offer in this battle against worry that is making people sick, and against fear that is scaring most of us half to death? It offers the greatest help of all. While the psychiatrist may counsel, and common sense may suggest, religion offers an unfailing solution and points to the specific means of achieving it. Our Christian faith lays down the fundamental principle which should be the solvent of all worries: Do the best you can. Then you have nothing to fear from God or man. Do your best and then with a good conscience leave the rest to God. Whether you succeed or whether you fail should cause you no concern, because you have done your best. More no one can do.

An Upright Life

Psychiatry, the science of mental hygiene, penetrates beyond this general principle and proposes three specific remedies. The first is this: Live a clean, upright life, and peace will hug your pillow. Like moths that wither under the sunlight, fear thrives in the dark places of character, in the secret closet wherein there dangles a family skeleton with the ever-present danger of being pulled out into public view. Bluebeard presents a poised exterior, but he quakes in his shoes before the ghosts of his clandestine amours. Every form of double dealing begets its secret dread.

Haunted by the ghosts of his embezzlements and double-dealing, Ivar Krueger, with palatial yachts, with summer homes in five countries, with millions of dollars deposited in his name, seizes his pearl-handled revolver and shoots himself in his luxurious suite in Paris. No army of liveried servants or bodyguards could ward off the invasion of the ghosts of his secret thefts.

Some years ago there came to the church office a young man whom I recognized at once as a prominent student on the campus of a state university.

"Father," he said, "I'm sitting on the top of a volcano, and the lid is liable to blow off any time."

"What do you mean?" I asked.

"Why," he replied, "I'm strutting about in the limelight of popularity, enjoying the friendship and esteem of the student body. But," he continued, "I feel like a hypocrite that's leading a double life. Sooner or later the mask will be pulled off and they'll know what I really am."

As we talked together, he told me that from the very beginning of his downward path he had not known one hour of peace or happiness. Remorse had proved an uncomfortable pillow. Worry and fear had dogged his footsteps.

He showed me a frayed newspaper clipping. It quoted his old coach as predicting he would be All-American before his senior year.

"Father," he said, "it isn't that I'm undermining my morale and throwing that chance away. What hurts me most, aside from the fact that I have offended my God, is that I've won the love of a good girl. She believes in me and trusts me. I suffer the tortures of the damned when I think of her finding out about my past and my none-too-steady present. I want to make a clean breast of it all and with God's help start anew."

As he stood before me, like a bronzed Apollo, with gleams of hope breaking at times through the clouds of fear and anguish mantling his countenance, I wished that I had the skill of a playwright to depict the drama being enacted before me. Lifting his tear-dimmed eyes toward heaven, he cried out, in words I shall never forget:

"O God! Let me begin . . . again."

I led him to the confessional, as the first step in the path to win back his self-respect and lost manhood.

An Age-Old Cry

As the young man unfolded his story to me, I wondered:

Will youth ever learn from the experience of the past? Or will it learn only by the painful process of burning its own fingers? I thought of that distant scene which occurred at the very dawn of the race's history: Adam sinning against God and then feeling the pangs of fear. "I was afraid," he cried out ". . . and I hid myself." How ancient and how modern is this reaction of the human soul to the consciousness of guilt!

I thought of Macbeth, after he had stained his hands with the murder of his king. Every noise affrights him. Ghosts are lurking in the dark corridors ready to spring at him. He hears a voice crying: "Macbeth shall sleep no more!" Then a knocking. Terrified, he cries out:

> *Whence is that knocking?*
> *How isn't it with me, when every noise appals me?*
> *What hands are here? Ha! they pluck out mine eyes!*

Then he utters those tremendous words which reflect the sense of an overwhelming guilt:

> *Will all great Neptune's ocean wash this blood*
> *Clean from my hand? No, this my hand will rather*
> *The multitudinous seas incarnadine,*
> *Making the green one red.*

What a contrast is Lady Macbeth! She showers contempt upon her husband for his inability to throw off the sense of guilt. Upbraiding him for his soft-heartedness, she displays a stony front that gives no inkling of fear or remorse. But what a different picture she presents in the final act: her iron nerve is breaking; she sleeps poorly; she walks at night through the dark corridors, carrying a candle. The nurse is perplexed at seeing her arise at night to scrub and scrub her hand. At last, terrified and unable to wash the blood away, she cries out: "Out, damned spot! Out, I say! . . ." After more scrubbing, she exclaims: "Here's the smell of blood still: All the perfumes of Arabia will not sweeten this little hand. Oh! Oh! Oh!" Whereupon, a physician, who has been standing in the darkened corridor and watching this scene with amazement, comments:

> *Foul whisperings are abroad. Unnatural deeds*
> *Do breed unnatural troubles: infected minds*
> *To their deaf pillows will discharge their secrets.*
> *More needs she the divine than the physician.*
> *God, God, forgive us all!*

I know of no more powerful portrayal of the paralyzing effect of fear from unrepented sin in all the literature of the world than these two scenes from *Macbeth.* They echo the experience of the race through all the ages. They seem to say:

"Young men and young women, if you have a virtuous character, hold fast to it. If you have lost it, win it back. It is the jewel that passeth all price, the pearl that is richer than all our tribe. For among all the dire consequences of wrong doing, the worst on this earth is that an evil life is haunted by the ghost of a sleepless fear."

Faith in God

The second specific which psychiatry proposes for the conquest of fear is this: Have a deep and abiding faith in God. How paltry and inconsequential the things that frighten us become when once we realize that we are in the shadow of the everlasting arms capable of protecting us from every foe. "Why are ye fearful?" Christ asked of His Apostles when they feared the waves would overwhelm their bark. Then He pointed to the real cause of their fear when He added: "O ye of little faith." Fearing when I am with you!

"God and one," said Lincoln, "constitute a majority." With God on our side, we have nothing to fear.

Love for All

The third specific which psychiatry proposes is this: Have a constant love for all mankind. Carry about no grudges. Don't strike back. The pus pockets of hatred are the favorite breeding ground of strife, irritation, and worry.

"But, Father," said a person to me some time ago, "there are some people who have wronged me and hurt me deeply. Resentment rankles in me still. I can't forgive them, much less love them."

Two considerations are helpful here. First, the words quoted by St. Paul: "Vengeance is mine. I will repay, saith the Lord." We need not usurp God's prerogative of meting out punishment. Secondly, love here does not necessarily imply an emotional fondness, but the wish for their welfare and eternal salvation. It is not possible to have an emotional enthusiasm for all types of people. But it is possible to desire the welfare and salvation of every one. It is possible to pray that God will help them, and, if they are wrong, show them the error of their ways, and lead them to the living of the good life.

The second consideration is contained in the words of a man who once said to me: "Father, when I find myself hating a person who did me a grievous wrong, I get down on my knees and pray for him. It is the only way I can overcome the temptation to hate him. When I arise, I find a spirit of peace in my heart. And I find myself reflecting: That man injured me! How foolish! Why, the only one who can injure me is myself. If I have sense enough to bear it patiently and not to strike back with hatred, I'll convert it into merit." How true indeed!

"Love Casteth Out . . ."

"Love your friends and hate your enemies" was the practice of the pagans as it is of unredeemed human nature today. But Christ said: "Love your enemies, do good to them that hate you." It is not easy. But it is the distinctive mark of a true Christian. It begets the richest premium in peace of mind and true happiness, both in time and in eternity. When Christ said: "Perfect love casteth out fear," He epitomized for all mankind a volume of psychotherapy, which psychiatrists will be but unraveling for centuries to come.

All of us need to pray for strength to rise to the heights of the true Christian. We need to utter the words of Rosa Marinoni in her *Plea for Greater Strength:*

I do not want
The bravery of those

Who, gun in hand,
Rush forth to slay their foes.
Not hatred, greed,
Or glory of conquest
Would I find rooted
In my human breast.
But this, O God, I ask:
'Please make me strong
To offer love to those
Who do me wrong.'

Past Mistakes

In addition to the specific remedies which psychiatry proposes for the conquest of fear, it should be pointed out that many of the worries which afflict mankind arise from the reflection upon past mistakes or misfortunes. There is a wide-spread tendency to cry over spilled milk, to lament mistakes long past, which no amount of lamentation can undo. Why worry and fret over past mistakes, when such fretting only robs one of the physical and mental strength to solve present problems? Persons who made unwise investments and sustained heavy losses will never recoup their losses by any amount of grieving and regretting.

True, people should profit by their past mistakes. They should not, however, allow them to become a source of constant misery, depleting their energy and robbing them of the initiative to try again. Instead of merely repeating the doleful words, "Of all sad words of tongue or pen, the saddest are these: 'it might have been,'" they might follow a more rational procedure and add this suggestion to the verse: "it might have been a great deal worse."

Needless Bridges

Even more prolific of worry than brooding over past mistakes is the chronic fear of future ills. We are constantly concerned over something which may happen, but which never does. We worry about the possibility of failing in our studies, in our business, in our social endeavors, in our work. We are continually building bridges for streams that never need to be crossed and climbing mountains that never beset our path; we are constantly imagining difficulties and envisaging misfortunes which we never actually have to face. "Most of our worries," as someone has aptly observed, "never happen."

To permit dark, melancholy thoughts over purely problematic difficulties and imaginary misfortunes to paralyze and cripple us is to convert life into a slow death. How true are the words of Shakespeare:

> *Cowards die many times before their death,*
> *The valiant never taste of death but once.*

The story is told of a soldier who was trembling like a leaf at the thought of what might happen to him when the signal sounded for his battalion to go over the top. A braver comrade calmly counseled:

"What, after all, is there to worry about? One of two things will happen. You are either going to be shot or to escape unhurt. If you escape, then there is nothing to worry about. If you are wounded, one of two things will happen. Either you will be mortally wounded, or you will recover. If you recover, then there is nothing to worry about. If you don't recover, then all your worries are ended."

This matter-of-fact analysis of all conceivable possibilities serves to characterize much of the purely anticipatory and imaginary anxieties which are making psychopaths and neurotics out of so many people today.

Roots of Worry

Worry often has its roots, psychiatry tells us, either in physical weakness or in mental maladjustments. If a person is "run down" and his nervous energy depleted, he lacks the proper resistance to worry and is much less capable of expelling it after it has entered. He becomes the easy prey to a host of phobias, hallucinations, obsessions and complexes which fight vigorously the attempts to expel them. They interfere with digestion, disturb the sleep, and further lower the body's resistence to other diseases.

Mental maladjustments constitute a still more prolific source of worry. Persons who are introverts, constantly turning their thoughts in upon themselves rather than upon the external world, are especially susceptible to habits of worrying. "A great need today," said a distinguished psychiatrist, "is self-decentralization."

Most of us are too self-centered. We make ourselves and our petty concerns the center of the universe; everything else in the universe revolves around our trivial cares. We become petulant and querulous if the entire cosmos does not bow to our whims and caprices. Our only interest in other things is indirect, namely, how they affect our happiness and well-being. Our world is egocentric, and, whenever things do not go our way, we are angry at the universe for not adjusting itself to our wishes, without suspecting that it is we who might well do the adjusting.

The habit of brooding over our troubles tends not only to aggravate and prolong our worries but also to endanger our mental health as well. In shying away from the realities of life, we build private worlds within our minds into which we withdraw in increasing measure. We allow our feelings and emotions to people it with characters of their own creation. The phantasies of our dream world become increasingly real, while the objective realities of life fade into wraith-like unrealities. The wholesome corrective which comes from the rubbing of shoulders with the grim realities of the external universe, which keeps us normal, is lacking.

As a result, we become singular and queer. The psychiatrist has more complexes to straighten out, more tangles to unsnarl. We need to reflect upon the wise proverb of the ancient Chinese: "The legs of the stork are long; the legs of the duck are short. You cannot make a stork's legs short, nor a duck's legs long. So, why worry?"

Things Worth While

The remedy for self-centralization is to think less of ourselves and more of others, to become absorbed in some transcending cause which makes our petty troubles sink into insignificance and gradually be forgotten. Instead of introverts we must become extroverts, focusing our interest upon the external world, instead of brooding on our own likes and dislikes and forever mulling over our subjective reactions to life's colorful drama. Athletes have been know to be so intent upon helping the team to win a victory that they were not conscious of bruises and hurts until after the contest. Persons who become passionately devoted to a great cause forget themselves and find that in struggling for a noble enterprise their worries fade into a happy oblivion. It is one of life's paradoxes that in pursuing happiness we miss it, while in forgetting about ourselves and seeking to bring happiness to others we find it.

Even more than psychiatry, religion helps a person to achieve a proper prospective in life, to secure a sense of values. What are the things which occasion so much worry? Are they not, for the most part, such things as the loss of money, the inability to "keep up with the Joneses," the necessity to get along without a servant, or to move to humbler quarters? What trivial mundane things these are, after all!

The Christian knows that, even though he lose all these treasures so highly prized in a materialistic age, he can still achieve the supreme values of life—unsullied character, noble manhood, virtue and kindliness—which never cease to win the honor, esteem and love of friends. With all the losses which a world economically awry can inflict on one, there is still enough to make life worth while—wife, children, friends, self-respect, spotless character, noble aspirations, high endeavors, above all, unbroken friendship with God.

These are the values which challenge us each day and fill life with the thrill of adventure and the bright colors of romance. Their achievement is dependent not upon the whims of external circumstances, but solely upon ourselves. The achievement of the supreme values of life challenges us to throw off fear, with its paralyzing effect, scaring us stiff and making us die many times before our death. It summons us to leave the slum district of the mind, with its black pessimism and haunting fears, and climb to the mountain peaks where the air is fresh and pure and bathed in the sunlight of heaven. "He has not learned the lesson of life," says Emerson, "who does not every day surmount a fear."

We do not seek to lift ourselves, however, merely by tugging at our bootstraps. We do our best and then appeal to the unfailing assistance of Almighty God. St. Paul reflects the secret of his amazing courage in confronting a hostile world and in reshaping its faith. "I can do all things," he says, "in Him that strengtheneth me." It is that Divine Being in whom the Apostle found strength who speaks again to a world, frightened and disturbed. "Why are you fearful, O ye of little faith?" In an upright life, an unfaltering faith, and a love that embraces enemies, mankind has not only a scientific but also a divine prescription for the conquest of fear and the achievement of that high courage of soul that looks out into the faces of men through eyes that are unafraid.

Summary

Every man and woman, no matter how obscure they are or how humble may be their work, are of supreme dignity and of transcendental value in the eyes of God. They are as precious and as dear to Him as are the kings and generals. All of us can invest our work with a divine significance by doing it in a spirit of dedication to Almighty God. It is this realization which will help all of us to achieve the courage to do our commonplace duties supremely well, to make them masterpieces in God's eyes, and thus attain a lofty serenity of soul and a peace of mind unsurpassed by that of kings or emperors.

RULE 10. *Do your daily tasks, no matter how prosaic and obscure, the best that you can; do them in a spirt of cheerfulness and dedication and leave the rest to God, knowing that God never fails to reward you for doing your best, regardless of whether men acclaim you a failure or a success.*

Reflect upon the instances of courage cited in this chapter and wait until tomorrow to read the next chapter.

Chapter Eleven

THE ART OF COURAGEOUS LIVING

Once more read thine own breast aright
And thou hast done with fears.
—Matthew Arnold, *Empedocles on Etna*

It will be helpful *to the reader if the various steps, methods, principles and considerations proposed through the preceding chapters for the development of courage are here briefly summarized and if a few of the psychological principles mentioned are further developed. Fear and courage are not opposites; they often exist in the same person at the same time. Fear is nature's method of alerting us to the presence of danger so that we can deal with it effectively. Fear has a twofold function: biotonic and educational. The first is concerned with the mobilization of the latent resources of the body to their maximum degree of power, vigor and endurance. The second function is to stimulate the mind to discover ways of circumventing the danger. It thus provokes the intellectual interests from which stem our science, art and philosophy.*

All normal men and women experience fear in the presence of danger. The few pathological individuals who lack this alerting and protective reaction are likely to be im-

prudent and foolhardy. Failing to weigh danger prudently, they take foolish risks and in consequence are apt to die young. Fear is the mother of prudence and man's invaluable ally in the struggle for survival, as well as for growth in knowledge and in wisdom.

Far from seeking to eradicate that protective reaction with which nature has endowed man, psychiatry uses it as the foundation for the development of prudent courage. A courage that faces the risks, weighs them intelligently, and then acts with despatch and determination is the only bravery worth while. Exaggerated and unfounded fear, apprehension, misgiving and anxiety are the enemies of courage and must be removed to safeguard the healthy emotional and mental life of man. But how? Here is where detailed practical guidance is necessary and invaluable.

Stop!

The first step is to face the disturbing situation frankly, calmly and with concentrated attention. Contrary to the suggestions offered by most people, "to forget about it," "to get it off your mind," psychiatry says: "Stop! Look! Listen!" Stop what you are doing and give your undivided attention to the problem or the situation which is disturbing you. To try to continue with other work will only mean that the disturbing element will be continuously jumping from the fringe of the focus of consciousness, stabbing you with fear and destroying the effectiveness of your work.

To try to flee from it is equally futile. Go to a party, a show, a dance, and it pursues you like a ghost. Its disturbing face is more vivid to you than that of the companion with whom you are endeavoring to converse; it clings to you like a leech, sucking your vigor and crippling your capacity to relax. Your smile is artificial and your laughter is forced; enjoyment has taken leave of you; anxiety has marked you for her own.

Look!

Look! Examine the disturbing situation. Analyze it carefully. Find out the specific element that frightens you. Fear thrives on the unknown; to localize a danger is half the battle. A commander sends out scouts to reconnoiter before his army advances. He wants to safeguard them against unseen and unexpected dangers; he knows that nothing is so likely to throw them into a panic as to be suddenly confronted with a danger for which they are unprepared.

Hormephobia, the intense dread of shock and surprise, can paralyze and glue them in terror to the ground. It is basic in all military strategy to reconnoiter the field of action, to investigate all dangers and to prepare for them effectively. Criminal indeed would be the negligence of a commander who would fail to explore the field of operation for concealed mines and hidden dangers that would take his troops by surprise and throw them into fear and panic.

"Knowledge," reports the National Research Council as a result of its study of fear, "is power over fear. Surprise is the most important element in battle. Thus, men should be kept constantly informed of the dangers they may meet, of the weapons that may be used against them, of the tactics which the enemy uses. Every moment of leisure should be used by the men to find out what they can about what the battle will be like, what the enemy is like. *The known is never so fearful as the unkown."*

Perhaps the most helpful knowledge is simply this: Every normal person experiences fear in the presence of danger. That is no sign of cowardice, and most individuals can overcome the fear. In the encounter with a disturbing situation, the individual must exercise similar vigilance to ferret out the element of danger, to isolate it from the tangled complex of circumstances and to prepare to meet it intelligently. Well does Matthew Arnold say:

The wiser wight
In his own bosom delves,
And asks what ails him so.

"A Bearded Man"

Let us illustrate the importance of this "look" phase of activity with a case occuring in our graduate work with the noted psychiatrist, Dr. Thomas Vernon Moore, at St. Elizabeth's Hospital, Washington, D. C. A patient of about thirty-five years of age reported that he was thrown into a tumult of fear whenever he saw a man with a Vandyke beard carrying a black satchel.

He was a sensible, educated man, and was at a loss to understand why such a sight would cause him such a paroxysm of terror. To get to the root of the fear we had to ask the patient to *look* back into his past life and try to recall when he first experienced such a violent seizure.

Step by step, he went back with our assistance until he recalled the first experience.

He was a boy of five when a physician was called to treat him for quinsy sore throat. Entering the dark room where the child was sleeping, the doctor flashed a light in his face, preparatory to looking into his throat. The child awakened, saw a strange, bearded face bent over him, and was terrified. Apparently, the doctor was lacking in bedside manners, and, without taking time to calm the boy, roughly opened his mouth and pushed an instrument into his throat.

The child was thrown into a paroxysm of horror, intensified by the fact that he had heard tales of a "Bluebeard" who strangled little boys who didn't obey. The fright left a psychic scar in the form of a strangulated emotion which had never been dissolved by an appropriate explanation. The memory of a bearded man with a black bag remained central in the terrifying experience. Years later, when the memory of the incident had long since passed away, the sudden appearance of a bearded man with a black satchel threw him into a convulsion of fear. This happened whenever he encountered such a sight. Why? He couldn't imagine.

"Swat the Mosquito"

Think how futile it would be to say to such a patient: "Forget about it." "Take in a show." "Get a couple of drinks." "Take a trip to a place where new scenery will wash the fear from your mind." Such a sight might be encountered anywhere. The recurrence of these convulsions was making him a nervous wreck.

By *looking* long enough and deep enough into his past, the man was able with our help to locate the origin of the fear and thus to release the strangulated emotion. The sunlight of reason, penetrating into this dark crevice of his youthful memory, was able to drive out the ghosts haunting him for years and rushing out in droves at the appointed signal — the sight of a bearded man with a black bag. The causes of most perturbing fears and dreads can be discovered only by looking frankly, calmly and with determined persistence into the perplexing situation.

Such fears are like the bites caused by a vexatious mosquito. To rub the sores may cause a momentary soothing of the irritation; but the annoying sores increase until the mosquito is tracked to its lair and killed. So will one's fears persist and grow until their cause is located and removed. "Swat the mosquito, not the sore" is the rule in public sanitation and hygiene. "Swat the cause of the fear, not the symptom" is the rule to be followed in the psychotherapy of banishing needless fears.

You will find it helpful in analyzing a situation and tracking down the disturbing element to write out your thoughts and feelings. Spend a half hour to an hour writing down everything that comes to your mind. Write with the utmost frankness and have the notes meant solely for your eyes. If necessary, continue this practice for several days. Then go over the writing, and you are likely to perceive some thread appearing with such frequency as to attract your suspicion. Follow that thread. Track it to its lair and you will find the source of the fear — the factor which throws you into unreasonable turmoil and makes you "see red." When finished with the writing, destroy the notes. They are intended to present a frank picture of your inner self, not a colored pastel with all the ugly marks painted out.

LISTEN!

The third item in this triple plan of attack is *Listen*! Listen to your whispered thoughts. Listen to the echo of your fears. Listen to the murmur of your secret dreads. Listen to the words which come unbidden to the mind and point like arrows to the hidden source of fear. Listen to what your dreams are trying to say to you.

We do not say that there is any need for the person disturbed by no obsessing fear or worry to pay attention to any and every dream. If he is deeply disturbed, however, the elements in the conflict are almost certain to act out the drama in his sleep. Here the mind continues to act, but with this important difference — the censorship of the will is released. The desires, cravings and aggressive tendencies suppressed during the consciousness creep out from their hiding places and have their fling. Hurling rebellion at the sleeping censor, they murder their hated foe or otherwise satisfy their organic cravings.

Thus, dreams are a form of disguised thoughts, mirroring a conflict between different elements of the personality. They are part of man's mental life and reflect his struggle to adapt himself to his real world. Frequently, they express a conflict between cravings for sexual gratification, for security, or aggressive tendencies on the one hand and the taboos and fears which block these cravings on the other.

In the dream, these elements are mixed; care must be taken to unscramble them. Inspection will disclose that at times the craving element will overshadow the context of the dream. Since the subject matter of dreams is closely related to the thoughts and acts of the day just ended, dreams may throw light on the subject's deep frustrations and rejected wishes.

"You throttled me during the day," they shout angrily at the sleeping will, at the moral ego, "but now we'll show you who's the boss." And they proceed to satisfy their frustrated yearnings.

It will not take an observer long to link up the dream with action in his daily life. This is particularly true when the individual is harassed by a disturbing fear. If he will but look at the drama enacted by his dream and *listen* to the recurring theme song of its actors, he will find a significant light thrown upon the problem of adjusting himself to the situation which has already flashed the danger signal of fear. He can use that light in tracking down the element staging the revolt in his dream life and throwing him into turmoil in his waking hours.

A Recurring Funeral

Let us illustrate. Ann reports to Dr. Moore that she is nervous, listless and subject to moods of melancholy. Questioning discloses that Ann is nearing her thirties; her mother is dead, and her father, an invalid, is the only other member of the family. She is well educated, of high moral character and of pleasing appearance. She devotes herself without stint to the care of her father.

What is the cause of her recurring moods of melancholia? It is not apparent on the surface. She is told to record her dreams and is given detailed directions as to how to note them. An examination of her dreams shows a pattern in which, strangely enough, the funeral of her father occurs repeatedly.

"Do you wish that your father would die?" she was asked, somewhat warily.

"Of course not," Ann answered indignantly. "I love my father and will stay and take care of him as long as he lives."

To desire her father's death was wrong, she knew, and so she repressed it as she did other thoughts and desires contrary to her moral code. Questioning revealed, however, that Ann was keenly conscious that she was losing out in her social life because of the duty of caring for her father. While other young girls were going out to parties and dances, she felt compelled to reject all such invitations so she could look after the invalid. Ann was not unmindful that the best years of her life, so far as getting married was concerned, were fast slipping by. The prospect was a disturbing one. She was caught between two pressures: the pressure of her conscience to stay at her post of duty and the pressure of deep biological urges and social cravings for marriage, children and a home of her own.

This was the conflict mirrored night after night in her

dreams. The repressed yearnings were going to secure their fulfillment by staging a funeral — the funeral of the father whose continued presence was blocking the path to their fulfillment. The conflict, so vividly and dramatically disclosed in her dreams — and solved with such deadly despatch — was showing itself in moods of melancholy, in a vague apprehension and in an indefinable disinclination to live. Unable to place her finger on the hidden cause of her malaise, she saw that her dreams pointed their fingers at it with a vengeance.

The Remedy

When the meaning of this recurring pattern in her dreams was explained to the young woman, she was quick to see its significance. Ann recalled the irritation she felt when she turned down invitations to parties. When, occasionally, she would find the wish that her father would die forming in her mind, she would instantly repress it. Driven deep into her subconscious mind, it would steal out during sleep and secure its fulfillment in her dreams.

The remedy was simple — to secure a nurse to relieve her in the evenings so she could have a normal social life. Four months later, she called on us. Ann was a changed person; her face was aglow with happiness. Her melancholia had disappeared, as well as her disinclination to live. The vague apprehension about her future, which had been disturbing her for several years and which had been increasing in intensity, had completely disappeared.

She was keeping steady company with a splendid young man a year or two her senior. The last we heard of her was when an invitation came a few months later, inviting us to her wedding. Because she had stopped, looked and listened, the vague fear about her future had been tracked to its hidden source. When the latter was removed, her fear, frustration and melancholia were replaced by the fulfillment of her dreams for love and happiness.

Capturing a Dream

"But I don't dream," some of you will say. "I dream," others will admit, "but very seldom." The fact is that you all dream, and do so every night; but many wake up abruptly at the rasping sound of an alarm clock, and pay little or no attention to what was in their mind at the moment they awoke. Hence, they do not recall their dreams and think they didn't dream at all. In passing from sleep to consciousness, a person enters a midway state, called the hypnogogic, in which he is partially awake and partially asleep. In that state he can seize whatever images and thoughts are in his mind and follow those threads back to the drama that was being enacted in his dream.

If one awakens gradually, he has a much better chance to glimpse the remnants of his dream than if he awakens to the furious clangor of an alarm clock, which startles him almost out of his skin. He will find it helpful to have a pencil and paper at his bedside so he can jot down immediately what is in his mind. The more elements of his dream he is able to seize at the moment of awakening, the easier it will be to recapture the whole dream. Helpful, too, will be an alarm clock with a soft gentle chime — why aren't there more? — which will lead him slowly and with understanding kindliness from the land of make-believe to the world of stern reality.

In most cases, a person can locate the hidden source of his apprehension by using the method of Stop! Look! Listen! Occasionally, however, there will occur cases where the fear has infiltrated so deeply into his mental life and has been of such considerable duration as to defy analysis by the individual. It will be advisable for such patients to secure the assistance of a psychiatrist.

It should be noted that the technique of self-study just outlined demands concentrated attention and sustained thought. It is no frivolous pastime; it means work, and plenty of it — but thinking is the most rewarding of all activities. Its dividends are never richer than those which free a person from obsessing fear and crippling anxiety. One who does so will find that his whole personality takes on a new lease on life; timid endurance is replaced with buoyant, confident living. This truth is reflected in the words of Matthew Arnold:

Resolve to be thyself: and know that he
Who finds himself loses his misery.

Anger and Aggression

In seeking to locate the secret cause of our fear, we can get some clues as to where to look from the findings of modern psychiatry. Research discloses that most of the secret fears of man cluster around three main drives or motivating forces, namely, anger and aggression, cravings for sex gratifications, and cravings for security. If we look behind the blanket of fear, we are likely to find our secret fears pitted against one of these deep-rooted urges or libidos.

Living in a closely knit society where every day we rub shoulders with others, we find many occasions of irritation. Our every-day speech is larded with expressions which mirror such vexation. We speak of "getting hot under the collar," "seeing red," "getting sore," "getting our dander up" and "getting peeved." While the policeman may prevent some individuals from expressing their anger, in the majority of cases the burden of such control rests on the mind itself.

Fear halts hostile acts before they get under way and may even efface the knowledge of hostile intent from the surface of the mind. Driven into the subconscious, the aggressive tendency loses the memory of its target, but persists in the form of a surly grouchiness, a suppressed rage, a blind fury, which blazes forth at the most unexpected moments. Soon, the individual finds that fears and apprehensions are mushrooming and filling him with misery and dread. To locate the hidden source of his fear the individual will have to use the method of self-study, the technique of Stop! Look! Listen! He will have to discover the true target of his animosity and find means of dissipating it.

The Sex Drive

Rooted in deep instinctive cravings, sex constitutes a powerful force in human life. The conflict between its drive and the efforts to restrain it has left scars on every personality. While powerful and persistent, sex is outranked in dominance by the drive of hunger, thirst, pain and fatigue, but the reason why sex is one of the most clamorous and dangerous impulses is because it is so frequently attacked and is the least gratified. Society attaches no penalty to eating, drinking, fleeing from pain, or discontinuing work if one is exceedingly tired, but there are long years when the sex drive must be borne with no hope of gratification.

The resistance generates a tension which produces unpleasant bodily feelings, prompting the individual to reach out in a blind, groping manner for relief and satisfaction. The repression of these urges may blur the conscious memory of what the individual is hungering for and may elicit vague fears and anxieties clustering around the struggle to control their unconventional expression. The whole story of the psychotherapy of sex is too long to recount here and would take us too far afield. Suffice it to make two observations:

First, much can be accomplished through intelligent sex instruction, starting as soon as the child becomes conscious of the endowment and curious about its purpose. Second, training in shepherding one's thoughts, prudence in avoidance of occasions which subject the endowment to too great pressure and the directing of its energy into socially useful channels, until its exercise in the family relation gives it meaning and purpose, are the means which will enable an individual to mature into a well-integrated personality possessing poise and self-control. Our purpose in referring to the sex drive here is simply to indicate a prolific source of hidden fear and anxiety, to which the individual might well direct his attention.

Craving for Security

The third powerful craving is for security. The conflict between the yearning for security and fears of insecurity are tearing at millions of people today, searing their personalities with battle scars.

Any storm cloud on the horizon threatening our future well-being causes uneasiness, concern and deep apprehension. Basic in the yearning for security are the simple, elemental needs of human life — the need for food, shelter, clothing, freedom from pain and escape from excessive fatigue. The prospect of going hungry, ragged, cold and in pain flashes the danger signals of fear and anxiety. Even when repressed from our minds they gravitate down in the cellar of our subconsciousness and fill us with a vague uneasiness and a groping discomfort which ever and anon flare up in agonizing tensions.

Often, the fear of insecurity is found to stem back to the days of infancy. Unable to express his wants, an infant is dependent upon adults to minister to his needs. Sometimes the adult is slow in coming or is unable to determine what the baby needs. Thus, the infant experiences the pain of these unsatisfied drives for food, drink, warmth, and escape from pain. Such painful frustrations are recorded in the personality and generate a feeling of apprehension which may flare up whenever similar danger signals appear.

Inferiority feelings are usually born in a sense of insecurity. Inferiority feelings may arise from the crude, ignorant or inconsiderate treatment of the child in the home. Parents who treat the child with too great severity, who scold him at every little slip he makes and who fail to lavish their love and kindness upon him are crippling him with a serious inferiority complex. The latter may also appear in the adult who finds himself in a society in which the majority of the others are better educated, have better manners and are better off financially. Comparing himself with these people on such points, he experiences a sense of inadequacy. Such feelings of inferiority are sometimes generated in marriages between persons of widely different social and cultural planes, and occasionally lead to estrangement and divorce.

In tracking down the hidden source of fear and anxiety, an individual will do well, then, to scrutinize the three most prolific sources — anger and aggression, the craving for sex gratification and the craving for security.

Do the Thing Feared

The way to learn to do a thing, psychology tells us, is to *do* it. The way to learn to swim is to practice swimming; the way to overcome a fear is to do the thing we fear to do. A person is afraid to venture deep enough into the water to try to stroke without hitting the bottom. Most people who never learn to swim probably fail because they are afraid to lift their feet off the bottom and recline in the water. They way for an individual to overcome such an irrational fear is, with the encouragement and assistance of a friend, to go deep enough into the water to go through the motions of swimming without constantly hitting the bottom. The oftener he does this, the faster will the fear disappear. Actually, swimming is one of the simplest of all operations. The slowness of most people in learning is due simply to their slowness in overcoming the fear to try to recline in the water and move their arms and legs.

Psychiatry assures us then that the way to overcome a foolish fear of doing something is to do that very thing and to do it often. A child is bitten by a dog. The resulting fright tends to make him fearful of all dogs; he may even fly into a panic when he sees a dog approaching him. The way to overcome the fear is not simply to tell him that not all dogs will bite, nor simply to have him observe how other boys play with dogs and are not hurt. Such general treatment must be followed by the specific act feared. He must stroke the head of a gentle dog, fondle him and play with him; every time he does that, he is dissipating the fear that otherwise would cripple him for life.

This psychological principle is reflected in the familiar proverbs: "Nothing ventured, nothing gained." "If at first you don't succeed, try and try again." "Practice makes perfect." Every successful performance of the feared act generates pleasure, re-establishes confidence and renders easier its next execution.

Action Dispels Fear

The studies of the National Research Council show that fear is at its height in time of suspense. Soldiers report that, when they were all set to lauch an attack, waiting for the signal to send them into action, they were nervous and jittery. The longer they were held in that state, the deeper did fear bite into them. Athletes have told us that they, too, are most on edge while waiting for a crucial game to begin; once they swing into vigorous action, their fears are dissipated. They are so absorbed in what they are doing that they do not have time to think of the dangers which previously had gripped their minds.

The psychological principle, *action dispels fear,* is especially applicable in the domain of war and of athletic sports where the foe is known. It is entirely compatible with the "Stop! Look! Listen!" procedure which is necessary to enable one to isolate the hidden source of fear in a vaguely disturbing situation.

Divert Attention from Fearful Aspect

Fear cannot be overcome by direct opposition. The affirmation, "I am not afraid," carries its own negation. When a parent counsels his child, "Now, don't be afraid," he unwittingly conveys to the child the idea that there is something to be afraid of. Instead of telling a child they won't hurt him, dentists find it more effective to divert his attention to something else. While telling him a story, they have slipped in the forceps and extracted the tooth.

Especially helpful is it to divert a person's attention to a humorous aspect of the situation. Because laughter entails the complete preoccupation of the mind by the humorous aspect, it excludes all other thoughts and feelings and is therefore an excellent antidote for fear. The heartier the laughter, the more complete is the banishment of fear. No medicine compounded by a pharmacist is half so effective in removing tension as a vigorous belly laugh. It is the unfailing remedy for apprehension, anxiety and dread. When its therapeutic value is more widely recognized, it will be cultivated more generally.

An army officer relates how a hearty laugh proved a lifesaver in a critical situation in World War I. His men were new recruits and were getting their first combat experience. They had taken shelter in a roadside ditch from the shell fire of the enemy, when, suddenly, they were filled with terror. The fire of American guns had been turned on them by mistake. Panic and horror were spreading among them. "Panic," reports the officer, "sent the blood pounding into my head and emptied my stomach of courage." Something had to be done and done quickly. Captain Wass did it. Unintentionally, but he did it.

"Jackson," he yelled.

"Yes, Captain."

"Where are you?"

"Right here — across the road."

"Stand up so I can see you."

"Captain," shouted Jackson above the crackling roar of machine-gun bullets, "if you want to see me, *you* stand up."

Smothered chuckles ran down the line. The tension of horror was snapped. Orders were given and listened to. Men wriggled backwards out of the zone of fire. The first to reach the trees dashed back to the gun post, which redirected its shells. A hearty laugh had saved the day — and countless lives as well.

Focus Attention upon Worthy Motive

There may be situations where even a thorough-going humorist can find nothing to laugh at. We can imagine that the American soldiers enduring the long siege at Corregidor, suffering hunger, dysentery, and extreme privation, and witnessing their comrades dying every day, found few, if any, occasions for hearty laughter.

In all such situations it is important to focus one's attention upon the ideal for which one is struggling and to attach one's self, heart and soul, to that ideal. In dedicating himself to a noble cause that transcends his aches and pains and his very life, a person finds an incentive to carry on in the face of hardship and affliction. Though the absorption with such a lofty and noble cause may not enable the individual to banish fear, it will give him the strength to bear it manfully. That is courage.

Take the early Christian martyrs who suffered torture and death rather than deny their faith. The sight of the lions waiting to devour them, of the swordsman waiting to behead them, of the cross on which they were to be crucified, could scarcely fail to arouse fear. They were able to endure their fear with sturdy fortitude because they were devoted to a cause of transcendent importance, for which they were willing to sacrifice their fortunes and their lives.

This is the meaning of decentralization. It is the remedy against the obsessing fears and crippling anxieties which spring from being wholly wrapped up in one's petty self. Self-centeredness generates pusillanimity, untrasensitivity to one's aches and pains, selfishness and moral cowardice. "The remedy," as the psychiatrist, Dr. T. A. Williams, has pointed out, "is the realization that one's own part in the great scheme of things is not of transcendent importance, and that to fulfill one's obligations is a greater thing than to avoid pain."

Narrow the Focus of Fear

Fear at first clings to a painful action, an unpleasant happening, a humiliating experience. But, like an infection, it tends to spread quickly. You have an unpleasant experience with Mr. Smith; the matter comes to court; your dislike spreads to Smith's attorney, to his family, to his friends, and ultimately to everything intimately associated with Smith. It may extend even to the color of the suits which Smith habitually wears or the distinctive eyeglasses he uses.

The cause of the dislike and resentment of many of these associations may never have been consciously adverted to; but, even if they had been, the memory soon becomes blurred and loses the connection. The result is that they become hidden sources of vague discomfiture and anxiety, spreading out in the subconscious from the original focus of the hatred and fear of Smith. Hence, it is important to confine the infection to its original focal point and extricate it. Otherwise, one's whole personality becomes saturated with irrational fears and resentments. To be angry and resentful of persons and things, without knowing precisely why, is particularly irritating and breeds a swarm of vague anxieties.

SUMMARY

RULE 11. *Confine the focus of fear and resentment to the smallest area. Try to eradicate it completely. Be on your guard against its spreading to associations, thus begetting irrational fears and vague anxieties.*

The other specific rules for the conquest of fear have been sufficiently developed in the previous chapters. A few basic general rules can be summarized briefly.

Do the best you can. No one can do more. Leave the rest to God. These two considerations will drain the pus pockets of worry and fear.

Live a clean, upright life. A good conscience is the best antiseptic for fear and anxiety.

Don't brood over past mistakes. Let the dead past bury its dead. Profit by the mistakes of the past. But face the living present and make a success of that.

Don't worry yourself sick over vague possibilities as to what may happen in the future. Everyone builds more bridges than he can ever cross. Most of the things over which people worry themselves sick never happen. Dispel the fear of future ills by realizing that ninety-nine per cent of them won't happen and that, when the one per cent comes around, you will be able to take care of it, you will relish facing it like a man and will be able to convert it from a liability into an asset.

Bear no hatred. Leave the guilty to God. Love all mankind, even those who irritate and annoy you. Love them for the sake of God. See the image of God in the face of every person. Remember that God will reward you espe-

cially for loving those who hurt you and speak evil about you untruly. "Vengeance is mine," declares Almighty God. He will settle all acounts with justice. Keep yourself blameless. Remember that you do not differ from the heathen if you love only those who love you. You become a child of God only when you do more than strict justice requires, only when you love all men, even your enemies.

Have a deep and abiding faith in God. Turn to Him in humble and fervent prayer. Such cries for aid have never gone unanswered. The response may not always be in just the form we desire. But it is the answer of one who knows what is best for us. Listen to the conclusion reached by the National Research Council on cold, scientific evidence: "Nor must we forget the power of religious belief as an antidote to fear. When men get into a tight spot they pray. They pray hard and from the heart, and they feel better for it." Prayer works.

Faith in God is the only firm and abiding foundation for a satisfactory philosophy of life. It is God who gives reality to spiritual values, to ideals, and provides adequate sanction for the moral order. He is the sure guarantee that a life of honor, virtue, unselfishness, service and love for all will bring an eternal reward.

These are the considerations which will enable everyone to conquer needless fears, to endure necessary ones, and to live a courageous, successful and happy life.

HERE ENDS THE READING OF THIS BOOK

NOW FOR THE LIVING OF IT

Nihil Obstat:

THOMAS A. DILLON
Censor Librorum

Imprimatur:

✠ JOHN F. NOLL, D.D.
Bishop of Fort Wayne

September 26, 1950

CHRISTOPHER PRESS, INC., ROCHESTER, N. Y.

AP 13 '67
AG - 3 '67